Harcourt

PHONICS
Practice Book
Copying Masters
Intermediate

Harcourt

Orlando   Boston   Dallas   Chicago   San Diego

Visit *The Learning Site!*
www.harcourtschool.com

CONTENTS

Unit 1: Consonants and Short Vowels

Unit 2: Long Vowels

Harcourt

Unit 3: More Work with Vowels

Harcourt

Phonics Practice Book

Unit 4: More Work with Consonants

Unit 5: Digraphs

Harcourt

Harcourt

Unit 8: Prefixes, Suffixes, and Agents

Cut-Out Fold-Up Books

Harcourt Brace School Publishers

Circle the letter or letters that stand for the beginning sound. Then write the letter or letters to complete the word.

1	k b t		2	c w p		3	d g r	
		___b___ear			___c___ar			___r___oad

4	z p s		5	w f x		6	m l g	
		___p___ig			___w___ater			___g___irl

7	t p h		8	j k n		9	z h v	
		___h___at			___j___ar			___z___ebra

10	p y l		11	f b m		12	b g r	
		___y___arn			___f___ish			___r___ope

13	br qu cl		14	b x l		15	p k d	
		___qu___een			___b___oy			___k___ite

     Initial Consonants   7

Name _____

Say the name of each picture. Circle the letter or letters that stand for the beginning sound. Then write the letter or letters to complete the word.

1 p (v) s
_____an

2 s b (t)
_____op

3 l f (s)
_____un

4 (m) n qu
_____ouse

5 p (l) z
_____og

6 n (p) k
_____ie

7 t (n) s
_____ail

8 (d) p v
_____og

9 p (qu) h
_____ilt

10 r (f) z
_____ox

11 (g) m p
_____ate

12 k l (j)
_____am

13 (m) b n
_____oon

14 l (k) y
_____ey

15 t p (h)
_____at

Harcourt Brace School Publishers

Name _____

1. van (circled) / man / tan
   van

2. 6 — mix / six (circled) / fix
   six

3. boat / goat (circled) / coat
   goat

4. mat / cat / hat (circled)
   hat

5. nut (circled) / hut / but
   nut

6. mean / queen (circled) / lean
   queen

7. gap / map (circled) / lap
   map

8. pig (circled) / big / wig
   pig

9. red / bed (circled) / fed
   bed

10. fan (circled) / man / can
    fan

11. sock / lock (circled) / dock
    lock

12. run / fun / sun (circled)
    sun

13. hot / cot (circled) / lot
    cot

14. bib (circled) / rib / fib
    bib

15. met / jet (circled) / pet
    jet

Write the word that best completes each sentence.

1. I will be ___ten___ years old on my next birthday.

        pen   bin   (ten)

2. John brought his ___bat___ to the baseball game.

        hot   (bat)   cob

3. The spider made a ___web___ in the corner.

        (web)   rob   bib

4. She used a ___pen___ to write the letter.

        hen   (pen)   tin

5. I hammered a ___nail___ into the wall.

        pail   sail   (nail)

6. John wiped his feet on the ___mat___.

        pat   sat   (mat)

7. The ___fox___ hid in a hole.

        box   (fox)   wax

8. Dad opened the ___jar___ of jelly.

        car   far   (jar)

9. Pam took a nap on a ___cot___.

        dot   (cot)   hot

10. The cat hit the ball of ___yarn___.

        barn   (yarn)   park

Name _____

Write the answer to each clue.

1. You use me to pick up leaves.

   My name rhymes with *bake*.

   _____ rake

2. You wear us on your feet.

   Our name rhymes with *rocks*.

   _____ socks

3. I am a farm animal,

   and my name rhymes with *jig*.

   _____ pig

4. I wear a crown, and

   my name rhymes with *seen*.

   _____ queen

5. I am a place to keep money.

   My name rhymes with *tank*.

   _____ bank

6. I shine in the sky at night.

   My name rhymes with *soon*.

   _____ moon

7. You do this to a soccer ball.

   It rhymes with *wick*.

   _____ kick

8. You use me when you eat.

   My name rhymes with *cork*.

   _____ fork

9. This is how snow feels.

   It rhymes with *hold*.

   _____ cold

10. Seven days make one of me.

   My name rhymes with *peek*.

   _____ week

Name _____

> **Use the letters below to complete each sentence. You may use some letters more than once.**

b	d	h	m	p	s	w
c	f	l	n	r	v	z

1. Our class took a bus trip to the __z__oo last __w__eek.

2. We took bag __l__unches and had a __p__icnic.

3. We saw a polar __b__ear and a __l__ion.

4. A __m__onkey was hanging from a __l__imb.

5. The __f__ox was hiding in a __h__ole.

6. We took a break on a __b__ench under a tree.

7. We drank glasses of __c__old __w__ater.

8. There were __m__any kinds of __d__eer.

9. We saw a __r__ed __b__ird in a tree.

10. We __v__isited the __r__eptile house.

11. We snacked on __m__elon and __b__ananas.

12. A train took us to see the __p__enguins.

13. The afternoon __s__un was very __h__ot.

14. We left the zoo at __f__our o'clock.

15. I took a __n__ap on the bus ride __h__ome.

Harcourt Brace School Publishers

Say the name of each picture. Circle the letter or letters that stand for the ending sound.

1	x s (ff) cuff	2	(l) t r tail	3	p (f) n leaf
4	(r) d l car	5	m (ll) zz bell	6	(mb) n t thumb
7	k (p) b cup	8	d k (t) foot	9	(n) m f crayon
10	p (g) s bug	11	k ff (x) fox	12	gg (ss) k glass
13	(k) x m hook	14	d p (b) web	15	b (d) n bed

Final Consonants 13

Circle the word that names each picture. Then write the word.

1. map
   man
   mad

   map

2. can
   cat
   cab

   cat

3. bin
   bat
   bib

   bib

4. lip
   lit
   lid

   lid

5. leak
   leaf
   lead

   leaf

6. six
   sit
   sip

   six

7. mill
   mitt
   mix

   mitt

8. cup
   cut
   cub

   cup

9. well
   web
   wet

   well

10. put
    pan
    pig

    pan

11. lamb
    lad
    lap

    lamb

12. click
    clip
    cliff

    cliff

13. dot
    dog
    doll

    dog

14. bead
    bean
    beak

    beak

15. jab
    jazz
    jam

    jam

Name _____

1. I am another name for *test*. _____
    quit   queen   (quiz)

2. I am part of your mouth. _____
    (lip)   lid   like

3. I am on the side of a mountain. _____
    clap   (cliff)   clip

4. I am between five and seven. _____
    sat   sit   (six)

5. I am another name for *lawn*. _____
    grab   (grass)   glue

6. I am something you can put on bread. _____
    (jam)   jar   pan

7. I am a game you can play. _____
    ten   (tag)   tap

8. I am where you go to learn. _____
    look   pick   (school)

9. I am a baby sheep. _____
    lamp   (lamb)   cat

10. I am the sound a bee makes. _____
    (buzz)   bun   bud

11. I come out when the sun sets. _____
    mood   mop   (moon)

12. I am part of a sandwich. _____
    broom   (bread)   beat

Say the name of each picture. Circle the word, and then write it.

1. bat
bad
(bag)

bag

2. (cat)
cab
can

cat

3. pad
(pan)
pat

pan

4. gun
(gum)
got

gum

5. (tub)
tug
tap

tub

6. end
ever
(egg)

egg

7. sub
(sun)
sum

sun

8. cob
cap
(cot)

cot

9. (leaf)
lead
leak

leaf

10. bat
bar
(ball)

ball

11. mate
mat
(map)

map

12. bud
(bus)
but

bus

13. (rug)
run
rub

rug

14. bet
(bed)
beg

bed

15. mill
mix
(mitt)

mitt

Harcourt Brace School Publishers

Fill in the circle next to the sentence that tells about each picture.

1		○ We used the mat to wipe our feet. ◉ We used a map to find the gold. ○ We were mad about the game.
2		○ Mrs. Jones rode a bike to work. ○ Mrs. Jones drove a cart to work. ◉ Mrs. Jones took a cab to work.
3		◉ Dad put a lid on the pot. ○ Dad put a light in the garage. ○ Dad lit the wood for the fire.
4		○ I will lead the band. ○ The sink has a leak. ◉ The leaf fell off the tree.
5		◉ Ann and Kay had a cup of tea. ○ Ann cut her knee today. ○ Ann and Kay saw a cub.
6		○ Jan drew a dot on the paper. ◉ Jan has a pet dog. ○ Jan has a paper doll.
7		○ The bird has a bead necklace. ○ The bird ate beans for lunch. ◉ The bird has a big beak.
8		◉ Dan stood on the cliff. ○ Dan put the clip on the papers. ○ Dan can click his fingers.

Use letters below to complete the sentences in the story. You may use some letters more than once.

p   m   k   d   n   g   t   x   w

The Jones family wen_t_ to a far_m_ near their tow_n_. Don and Pat

helped fee_d_ the chickens, the pigs, and the co_w_. Dad saw a ma_n_

mil_k_ the co_w_. Mom gathered eggs from the he_n_.

Mom and Pat made ja_m_ in a pa_n_. Don saw a little chic_k_ in a

bo_x_. Dad picked cor_n_ in the garde_n_.

For lunch, the Jones family ate corn, ha_m_, sala_d_, and warm bread

with honey. They had ice crea_m_ for dessert. Then Pat and Don played

ta_g_ in the yar_d_. Mom read a boo_k_ while Dad took a na_p_.

Say the name of each picture. Write the letter that stands for the sound you hear in the middle of the word.

1	2	3
ti_g_er	ca_b_in	spi_d_er

4	5	6
ru__l__er	ca_m_el	pea_n_ut

7	8	9
pa_p_er	sa__l__ad	wa_g_on

10	11	12
mo__n__ey	mu__s__ic	ba_b_y

13	14	15
le_m_on	wa_t_er	me_t_er

16	17	18
co__l__or	de_s_ert	pia_n_o

Write the word that answers each clue. You will not use all the words.

melon	desert	tulip	honey	wagon	baby
spider	paper	money	tiger	sweater	robin
camel	water	ruler	music	dragon	tuba

1. You can buy things with me.   _money_

2. You can draw on me.   _paper_

3. I am a fruit you can eat.   _melon_

4. I make a web.   _spider_

5. I taste very sweet.   _honey/melon_

6. You can ride in me.   _wagon_

7. Put me on when you are cold.   _sweater_

8. I help you draw a straight line.   _ruler_

9. You hear me on the radio.   _music/tuba_

10. My nest is in a tree.   _robin_

11. Drink me when you are thirsty.   _water_

12. I am a make-believe animal.   _dragon_

13. You can see me in a band.   _tuba_

14. I grow in the spring.   _tulip_

15. I am a hot, dry place that gets little rain.   _desert_

Harcourt Brace School Publishers

Fill in the circle next to the sentence that tells about each picture.

1	● Dad took Betsy to the zoo.
	○ Dad took the dragon to the zoo.
	○ Dad took the robin to the zoo.

2	● Dad found a spiderweb in the corner.
	○ Dad found a beaver in the corner.
	○ The spiderweb was on the tiger.

3	○ The camel swam in the river.
	○ They saw a camel in the desert.
	● They rode a camel around the park.

4	○ Dad and Betsy made some money.
	● Dad and Betsy listened to some music.
	○ Dad and Betsy were in a band.

5	○ Salad is good for lunch.
	○ A woman was on the bench.
	● They ate melon on the bench.

6	○ Betsy poured a glass of juice.
	○ A robin splashed in the water.
	● Dad helped Betsy get some water.

REVIEW Say the name of each picture. Write the missing letters to complete the words.

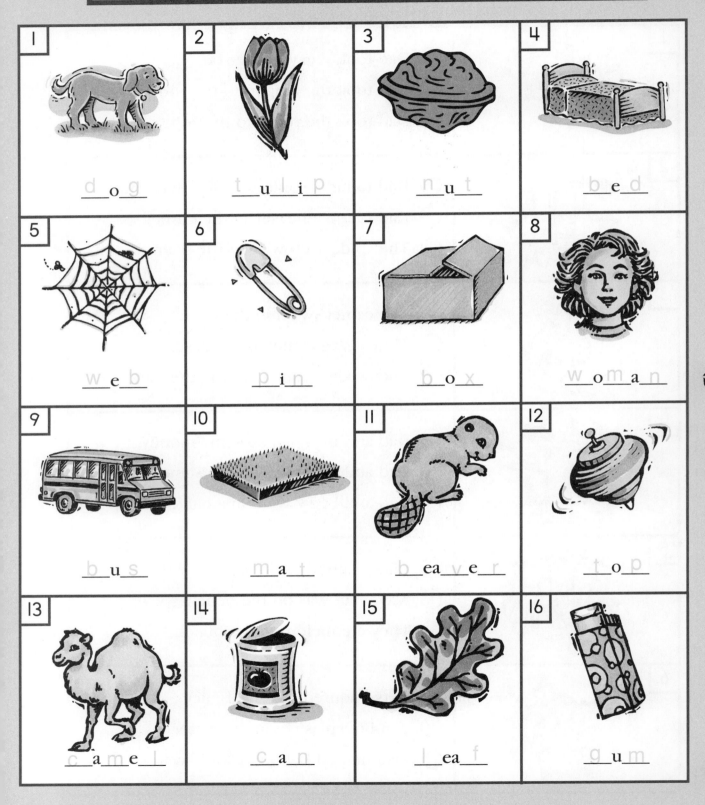

1. d _o_ _g_

2. _t_ u _l_ i p

3. _n_ u _t_

4. _b_ e _d_

5. w _e_ _b_

6. _p_ i _n_

7. _b_ o _x_

8. w _o_ _m_ a _n_

9. _b_ u _s_

10. _m_ a _t_

11. _b_ ea _v_ e _r_

12. _t_ o _p_

13. _c_ a _m_ e _l_

14. _c_ a _n_

15. _l_ ea _f_

16. _g_ u _m_

Name _____

Use the letters below to complete the sentences. You may use some letters more than once.

l   b   t   n   p   h   g   w   f   r   d   m

The Nolen __amily went to their ca__in near the lake. They __ulled their things up the steep __ill in a wa__on. Dad unlocked the doo__, and they all went inside. Dad saw a spi__er web by the __indow.

Carol and Judy walked down to the __ake. They ate some pea__uts. The __irls saw a __oman with __our children in a sai__ boa__ on the wa__er.

Later that __ay, the Nolen family ate sa__ad and ha__ for supper. They each had a slice of me__on. Then Mark played the pia__o. Everyone was happy after the __ong day.

Write the answers to the questions.

Possible responses are shown.

1. Where did the Nolen family take a trip to?_____

____their cabin near the lake____

2. What did the girls see at the lake? _____

____woman with four children in a sailboat____

Harcourt Brace School Publishers

Fill in the circle next to the word that names the picture.

1
- ○ wet
- ○ wed
- ● web

2
- ○ cob
- ● cot
- ○ cod

3
- ● bed
- ○ bet
- ○ beg

4
- ○ dot
- ● dog
- ○ doll

5
- ● top
- ○ mop
- ○ hop

6
- ○ lean
- ○ leap
- ● leaf

7
- ● camel
- ○ cable
- ○ cattle

8
- ○ sum
- ● gum
- ○ hum

9
- ○ hut
- ● hat
- ○ hit

10
- ● bell
- ○ sell
- ○ well

11
- ● box
- ○ fox
- ○ wax

12
- ● bus
- ○ bun
- ○ bud

13
- ○ bin
- ● pin
- ○ tin

14
- ○ cut
- ● nut
- ○ rut

15
- ○ cab
- ○ cart
- ● cat

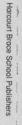

Fill in the circle next to the sentence that best tells about each picture.

1		○ Uncle Mac saw a cat at the zoo.
		◉ Uncle Mac saw a zebra at the zoo.
		○ Uncle Mac saw a seal at the zoo.

2		◉ Pat and Sam saw a crab at the beach.
		○ Pat and Sam saw a crow at the beach.
		○ Pat and Sam saw a crown at the beach.

3		○ Dan and his mother took cookies to the party.
		○ Dan helped his mother play music.
		◉ Dan helped his mother toss the salad.

4		◉ Dad poured Ann a glass of milk.
		○ Dad made Ann a sandwich.
		○ Dad gave Ann some melon.

5		○ Grandmother baked a cake for Kate.
		◉ Grandmother made a quilt for Kate.
		○ Grandmother fixed the bike for Kate.

6		○ The chicken ate a seed.
		○ The chicken ran across the yard.
		◉ The chicken laid an egg.

7		○ We rode the cart down the hill.
		◉ We rode the sled down the hill.
		○ We rode the wagon down the hill.

8		◉ We like to play in the water on a warm day.
		○ We like to play in the sand on a warm day.
		○ We like to play in the cabin on a warm day.

m<u>a</u>t

b<u>a</u>t

If a word has only one vowel, and it comes between two consonants, the vowel is usually short. Write *a* to complete each word that has the short *a* sound.

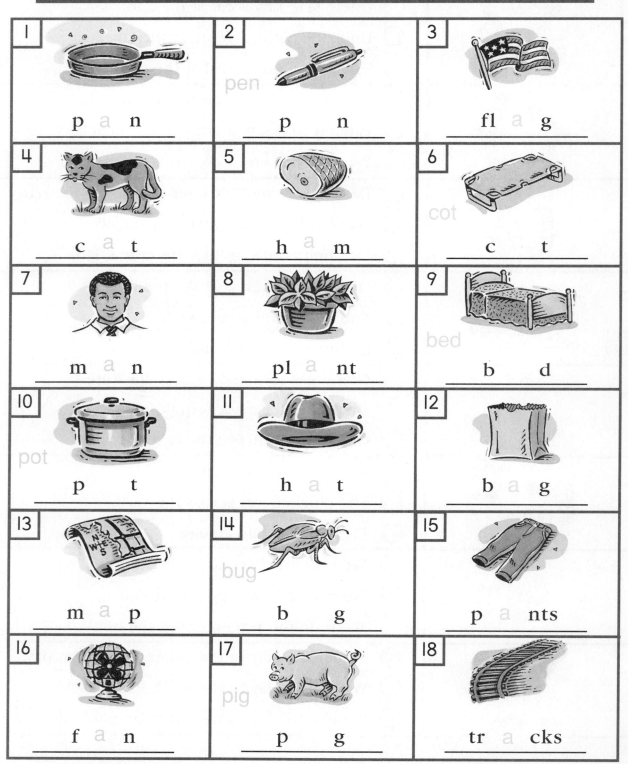

1. p <u>a</u> n

2. p __ n   *pen*

3. fl <u>a</u> g

4. c <u>a</u> t

5. h <u>a</u> m

6. c __ t   *cot*

7. m <u>a</u> n

8. pl <u>a</u> nt

9. b __ d   *bed*

10. p __ t   *pot*

11. h <u>a</u> t

12. b <u>a</u> g

13. m <u>a</u> p

14. b __ g   *bug*

15. p <u>a</u> nts

16. f <u>a</u> n

17. p __ g   *pig*

18. tr <u>a</u> cks

Circle the name of each picture. Then write the word.

1. pod
   paid
   (pad)

   _____

2. (hat)
   hit
   hate

   _____

3. pane
   (pan)
   pain

   _____

4. (cap)
   cape
   cup

   _____

5. fine
   fun
   (fan)

   _____

6. cane
   cub
   (can)

   _____

7. meat
   (mat)
   mate

   _____

8. (tack)
   take
   tuck

   _____

9. but
   (bat)
   bait

   _____

10. cape
    (cat)
    cot

    _____

11. rug
    rage
    (rag)

    _____

12. pans
    (pants)
    paints

    _____

Short Vowel: /a/a

27

Name _____

Write a word that rhymes with each picture name.

Possible responses are shown.

1  **cap** map, nap	**2**  **pad** sad, mad	**3** **bat** cat, flat
4  **lamp** camp, damp	**5**  **fan** ran, tan	**6** **ham** clam, jam
7 **tag** rag, bag	**8**  **tack** back, quack	**9**  **ax** tax, wax
10 **pan** can, Dan	**11**  **map** rap, tap	**12**  **hand** band, sand

28 Short Vowel: /a/ a • Phonograms

Name _____

Harcourt Brace School Publishers

Write the word from the box that completes each sentence. You will not use all the words.

> bat   pan   bait
> bag   pain   cap

1. Jack has his _____cap_____ .

2. Put the lid on the _____pan_____ .

3. Pam hands the _____bat_____ to Joan.

4. Dan has a _____bag_____ of apples for Ann.

> tuck   pad   tack
> mate   hat   mat

5. I wipe my feet on the _____mat_____ .

6. My _____hat_____ keeps my ears warm.

7. Mary writes her name on the _____pad_____ .

8. Kim uses a _____tack_____ to hang her ribbon.

Short Vowel: /a/a

Read the story and answer the questions.

The Picnic

Last summer the Frank family went on a picnic by a lake. Dad and Zack played in the water. Mom and Brad floated on a raft. Patty played in the sand.

They found a shady place to eat. They had ham, yams, and cans of juice. After lunch Zack and Brad took a nap.

Dad, Mom, and Patty played tag. They saw something black running in the grass. Patty tried to catch it. She tripped and fell. The fast black cat ran from her hands. The cat woke Zack and Brad from their naps.

The Franks went down to the lake. They saw tadpoles in the water. Then they drove home in their van.

Possible responses are shown.

1. What did the Franks do for fun on their picnic? They played in the water, floated on a raft, played in the sand, and played tag.

_____

2. What did the Franks eat for lunch?

ham, yams, and cans of juice.

_____

3. Why did Patty fall?

She tripped while trying to catch a cat.

_____

Harcourt Brace School Publishers

If a word has only one vowel, and it comes between two consonants, the vowel is usually short. Write *e* to complete each word that has the short *e* sound.

b**e**d

1 p___g	**2** b___t	**3** p_e_n
4 b___x	**5** w_e_b	**6** f_e_nce
7 ch_e_ck	**8** s___n	**9** t_e_n
10 sh_e_ll	**11** d___g	**12** d_e_sk
13 h_e_n	**14** v___n	**15** v_e_st
16 n_e_ck	**17** b_e_lt	**18** c___p

Name _____

1.

pear

(pen)

pet

pen

2.

bet

bead

(bed)

bed

3.

(net)

neat

near

net

4.

cheap

(check)

cheek

check

5.

teen

tent

(ten)

ten

6.

shall

(shell)

shut

shell

7.

steep

stop

(step)

step

8.

(well)

wheel

will

well

9.

bunch

beach

(bench)

bench

10.

teen

tint

(tent)

tent

11.

(wet)

wheat

with

wet

12.

(jet)

jack

jab

jet

Write a word that rhymes with the name of each picture.

Possible rhyming words are shown.

1	bed	2	tent	3	pen
	fed, red		dent, rent		den, men
4	bell	5	egg	6	men
	fell, sell		leg, beg		then, hen
7	vest	8	well	9	leg
	best, rest		shell, tell		beg, peg
10	bench	11	dress	12	hen
	French, wrench		mess, press		pen, men

Look at the pictures above. Do what the sentences tell you.

Accept reasonable pictures.

1. Draw a pet on the bed.

2. Draw more men.

3. Draw a fence next to the tent.

4. Draw a bow on the vest.

5. Draw a hen by the pen.

6. Draw a pet with four legs.

7. Draw a jet over the well.

8. Draw one more hen.

9. Draw a nest under the egg.

10. Draw a belt on the dress.

Harcourt Brace School Publishers

Write the word that completes each sentence. You will not use all the words.

| Red | pen | put | pet | fed |

1. Jeff got a dog for a _____ pet _____ .

2. Jeff said, "I will call you _____ Red _____ ."

3. Jeff _____ fed _____ his dog a snack.

4. Jeff made a _____ pen _____ for Red in the yard.

| bed | Teen | beg | Ten | led |

5. Jeff showed Red how to _____ beg _____ .

6. Jeff _____ led _____ Red on a short walk.

7. Jeff made a _____ bed _____ for Red.

8. Jeff said, " _____ Ten _____ o'clock. Time for bed."

Harcourt Brace School Publishers

Name _____

Ned and Ted's Hike

Ned went for a hike with Ted,
Up and down where the path led.
They saw a spider in a web,
And a boy whose name was Jeb.
They saw a red bird in a nest,
And a girl called Jen in a vest.
They saw a bug with six black legs
And a hen with lots of eggs.
They saw a fox outside its den,
And some rabbits in a pen.
Then Ned and Ted went home to rest
And tell Aunt Meg what they liked best.

JEB

1. What did Ned and Ted see on their hike? a web, a boy named Jeb, a red bird in a nest, a girl called Jen in a vest, a bug with six legs, a hen, eggs, a fox outside its den, and some rabbits in a pen

2. What did Ned and Ted plan to do when they got home?
They planned to rest and tell Aunt Meg what they liked best.

Now circle all the words in the poem that have the short *e* sound.

Name _____

Write the word that names the picture.

1 map	2 bed	3 hen
4 bag	5 pen	6 van
7 men	8 ham	9 ten
10 leg	11 cat	12 bat
13 web	14 hat	15 belt

Name _____

Write the word that answers each clue. You will not use all of the words.

REVIEW

jam   ten   pan   pen   cap   cup   cab   bed   tan

1. You can ride in it. _____cab_____

2. We eat it on bread. _____jam_____

3. It comes after nine. _____ten_____

4. You can write with it. _____pen_____

5. You wear it on your head. _____cap_____

6. You can sleep in it. _____bed_____

bet   smell   stem   bat   red   stream   fast   bell   reed

7. You hit a ball with it. _____bat_____

8. You hold this part of a flower. _____stem_____

9. It tells how some people run. _____fast_____

10. It is a color in the American flag. _____red_____

11. You hear it ring. _____bell_____

12. You do this with your nose. _____smell_____

Name _____

If a word has only one vowel and it comes between two consonants, the vowel is usually short. Write *i* to complete each picture name that has the short *i* sound.

m**i**tt

1. p__i__g	2. car c____r	3. l__i__d
4. h__i__ll	5. lamb l____mb	6. l__i__p
7. web w____b	8. d__i__sh	9. r____ng
10. van v____n	11. f__i__n	12. ch____n
13. bat b____t	14. b__i__b	15. s____x

Harcourt Brace School Publishers

Write *yes* or *no* to answer each question.

| 1 | Is the baby wearing a bib? |
| | _____ yes _____ |

| 2 | Did Kip see six pigs at the farm? |
| | _____ no _____ |

| 3 | Did Kim hit the ball? |
| | _____ yes _____ |

| 4 | Do fish swim in a pond? |
| | _____ yes _____ |

| 5 | Did Jim have his mitt? |
| | _____ yes _____ |

| 6 | Can a tree have a limb? |
| | _____ yes _____ |

| 7 | Is Mindy with the other kids? |
| | _____ no _____ |

| 8 | Does the wig fit on Ginny's head? |
| | _____ yes _____ |

| 9 | Did the dog dig the hole? |
| | _____ yes _____ |

| 10 | Are the pins in the bin? |
| | _____ yes _____ |

Name _____

Write a short *i* word to answer each question.

1. What lives on a farm and rhymes with *big?* _____ pig

2. What lives in water and rhymes with *wish?* _____ fish

3. What do you drink that rhymes with *silk?* _____ milk

4. What goes on your head and rhymes with *pig?* _____ wig

5. What comes after five and rhymes with *mix?* _____ six

6. What goes on a pan and rhymes with *kid?* _____ lid

7. What part of your mouth rhymes with *dip?* _____ lip

8. What part of a fish rhymes with *win?* _____ fin

9. What can you walk to the top of that rhymes with *fill?* _____ hill

10. What part of your body rhymes with *tip?* _____ hip

11. What is the opposite of *small* and rhymes with *dig?* _____ big

12. What names a color and rhymes with *sink?* _____ pink

13. What fits on your finger and rhymes with *king?* _____ ring

14. What do you put food on? It rhymes with *fish.* _____ dish

15. What sound does a clock make? It rhymes with *lick.* _____ tick

Write the word that completes each sentence. You will not use all the words.

limb	sit	hill	with	mitt
tip	lip	hit	Bill	win

1 Will went up a _____ hill _____.

2 He took his ball and _____ mitt _____.

3 At the top of the hill, Will met _____ Bill _____.

4 He sat on a _____ limb _____ in a tree.

5 "Now we can play _____ with _____ my baseball," said Will.

6 Bill _____ hit _____ the ball.

7 "You _____ win _____!" said Will.

Read the story and answer the questions.

A TRIP TO THE BEACH

Jim and Jill went to the beach with their family. "We will sit here," said Mother. Jim and Jill began to dig in the sand. They made a big hill.

Jim and Jill saw six fish swim by. The fish had pretty red fins. "I wish I could swim like a fish," said Jill.

"You can sit here and dip your feet in," said Mother. Jill put the tip of her big toe in the water. "It is cold!" she said.

Baby Liz came to sit with Jim and Jill. Liz wore a pink bib. Jim scooped up some water and let it drip on her toes. That made Liz grin.

"It is almost six o'clock," said Mother. "It is time to go home for dinner."

Possible responses are shown.

1. Who took a trip to the beach? _____ Mother, Jim, Jill, and Liz _____

2. What did Jim and Jill do in the sand? _____ They made a big hill. _____

3. Why did the family have to go home? _____ It was almost six o'clock _____

and time for dinner.

Now underline all the short _i_ words in the story.

Harcourt Brace School Publishers

If a word has only one vowel and it comes between two consonants, the vowel is usually short. Write *o* to complete each picture name that has the short *o* sound.

t<u>o</u>p

1  f<u>o</u>x	**2**  h___t	**3**  d<u>o</u>ll
4  s<u>o</u>ck	**5**  w___b	**6**  r<u>o</u>ck
7  j___r	**8**  m<u>o</u>p	**9**  p___n
10  l___g	**11** 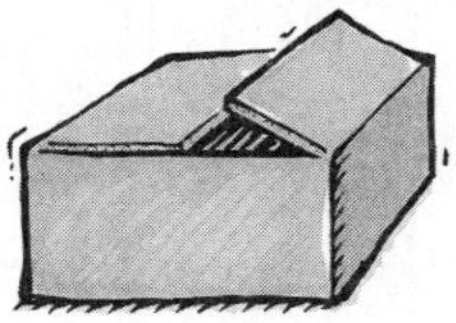 b<u>o</u>x	**12**  h___ll
13  h___n	**14**  p<u>o</u>t	**15**  cl<u>o</u>ck

Short Vowel: /o/o

Write *yes* or *no* to answer each question.

1		1. Can a fox sit on a rock? _____yes_____
2		2. Did Ross catch a cod with his fishing rod? ____no____
3		3. Could Rob buy a top at the toy shop? _____yes_____
4		4. Did Jan put her doll on the cot? _____yes_____
5		5. Does Tom sell boxes at his job? _____no_____
6		6. Did Donna drop her box? _____no_____
7		7. Is the pot on top of the stove? _____yes_____
8		8. Did the pot get hot? _____yes_____
9		9. Does this sign tell you to stop? _____yes_____
10		10. Is Bob taller than the clock? _____no_____

Write a word that rhymes with each picture name.

Possible responses are shown.

1 rock lock, sock	2 box fox	3 cot dot, got
4 top cop, hop	5 cob job, bob	6 log fog, hog
7 pond bond, fond	8 sock rock, dock	9 rod nod, pod
10 clock lock, dock	11 ox box, fox	12 pot lot, rot

Short Vowel: /o/o • Phonograms

Name _____

Write the word that completes each sentence. You will not use all the words.

> mop   cob   hot   Jon   mom
> pot   lock   stop   box   got

1. Jon went camping with his _____mom_____.

2. Jon got wood out of a _____box_____.

3. His mom built a _____hot_____ fire.

4. Jon _____got_____ out a pot and put water in it.

5. He set the _____pot_____ over the fire to get hot.

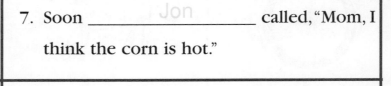

6. Then he added the corn on the _____cob_____.

7. Soon _____Jon_____ called, "Mom, I think the corn is hot."

8. It was hard to _____stop_____ eating that corn!

Short Vowel: /o/*o*

Phonics Practice Book

Name _____

Read the story. Then answer the questions.

The Top of the World

A frog hopped out of the pond. He hopped along, through the fog. The frog saw a dog on top of a rock. "What are you looking for?" asked the frog.

"I want to see the top of the world," said the dog.

The frog hopped on, into the bog. He saw a fox on a log. "What are you looking for?" asked the frog.

"I want to see the top of the world," said the fox.

The frog hopped on through the fog. He saw a bird on a limb. "What are you looking for?" asked the frog.

"I want to see the top of the world," said the bird.

The frog hopped to a spot on the dock. Then the sun came out and the fog went away. The frog saw the cool water and the blue sky. He felt the hot sun on his back. "This must be the top of the world," he said. Then he hopped back into the pond.

Possible responses are shown.

1. Who did the frog see as he hopped along?

   The frog met a dog, a fox, and a bird.

   _____

2. What did the dog, fox, and bird want to see?

   They wanted to see the top of the world.

   _____

3. What made the frog think he had found the top of the world?

   He saw the cool water and the blue sky.

   He felt the hot sun on his back.

   _____

Harcourt Brace School Publishers

Circle the letter that stands for the short vowel sound in each picture name.

1 box
a
e
(o)

2 log
e
(o)
i

3 hill
(i)
o
a

4 pig
e
o
(i)

5 mop
(o)
e
i

6 mitt
a
(i)
o

7 doll
i
(o)
e

8 pins
o
(i)
a

9 wig
a
(i)
e

10 fox
(o)
e
i

11 cot
i
(o)
a

12 clock
i
a
(o)

13 bib
e
(i)
o

14 sock
a
(o)
i

15 six
(i)
o
e

Harcourt Brace School Publishers

Circle the answer to each clue. Then write the word on the line.

1. It is part of your mouth. _____
   lip (lip) lap leap

2. You put this on your foot. _____
   sock sack (sock) sick

3. You need a key to open this. _____
   lock lake (lock) lick

4. This animal lives on a farm. _____
   pig (pig) peg pain

5. When you go camping, you sleep on this. _____
   cot (cot) cat cut

6. A baby wears this. _____
   bib bob (bib) bud

7. You hold this when you go fishing. _____
   rod rid red (rod)

8. You use a shovel to do this. _____
   dig dog (dig) dime

9. You can climb to the top of this. _____
   hill hall heel (hill)

10. This animal hops and likes the water. _____
   frog (frog) flip float

Name _____

The letter *u* often stands for the short *u* sound. Sometimes the letters *ou* stand for the short *u* sound. Write the word that names each picture.

cub   mug   rug   cuff   duck   tub   bus   bug

1. rug
2. bus
3. tub
4. duck
5. mug
6. cub
7. cuff
8. bug

Write the word that completes each sentence.
You will not use all the words.

young   stump   rough   stamp   earth   country

9. We sat on a tree ____stump____ .

10. A kitten is a ____young____ cat.

11. The ____rough____ waves rocked our boat.

12. The United States is the ____country____ we live in.

Short Vowel: /u/*u, ou* • Reading Words with Short *u*

Phonics Practice Book

The words below are hidden in the puzzle. Some words go across. Some words go down. Find and circle each one.

tub   pump   duck   truck   drum   tough   gum
thumb   puppy   rough   sun   cousin   bug   rust   double

r	o	u	g	h	c	p	h	d	e	d	m	p
u	a	x	u	t	z	t	u	b	b	o	g	u
s	u	n	m	e	t	h	d	l	p	u	m	p
t	d	r	b	c	o	u	s	i	n	b	f	p
b	r	j	o	k	u	m	a	u	i	l	j	y
d	u	c	k	f	g	b	u	g	c	e	i	w
q	m	n	h	s	h	g	t	r	u	c	k	v

Write the name of each picture.

1 gum	2 duck	3 tub
4 sun	5 bug	6 truck

Name _____

Write the word that completes each sentence. You will not use all the words.

Sue	bus	plum	bump	duck
trip	cousin	Gus	snow	under	lunch

1

_____ Gus _____ went to school.

2

He rode on a big _____ bus _____ with many other children.

3

Gus saw a _____ duck _____ swimming in a pond.

4

The bus went over a _____ bump _____ in the road.

5

At school, Gus saw his _____ cousin _____.

6

They sat _____ under _____ a tree to eat.

7

Gus had some juice with his

_____ lunch _____.

8

He pulled out a ripe, purple

_____ plum _____.

Harcourt Brace School Publishers

Write the word that answers each question.

1. What covers the floor and rhymes with *mug*? _____ rug

2. What has a shell and rhymes with *cut*? _____ nut

3. What shines in the sky and rhymes with *fun*? _____ sun

4. What makes a good pet and rhymes with *guppy*? _____ puppy

5. What says "quack" and rhymes with *luck*? _____ duck

6. What has six legs and rhymes with *jug*? _____ bug

7. What is a part of your hand and rhymes with *crumb*? _____ thumb

8. What can you drink from that rhymes with *bug*? _____ mug

9. What means "two" and rhymes with *trouble*? _____ double

10. What is the opposite of smooth and rhymes with *tough*? _____ rough

Read the story, and answer the questions.

Buff, the bear cub, went for a walk in the woods to look for bugs. He saw a duck in a pond, but he did not find any bugs. He saw bright red berries, but he did not find any bugs. He saw nuts on a tree, but he did not find any bugs. He saw a gull in the sky, but he did not find any bugs.

Buff walked on. A big buck jumped across the path. Then Buff walked in the mud and came to an old hut.

Buff rubbed his back against a tree stump. The bark felt rough on his back. Then Buff rolled down a hill, thumping and bumping until he hit a rock.

When Buff got up, he saw bugs under the rock. He dug up the bugs and ate them. There were just enough. Then Buff curled up and took a nap.

Possible responses are given.

1. Why did Buff go for a walk?

went to look for bugs

2. What did Buff see while he was looking for bugs?

a duck, berries, nuts on a tree, a gull, a buck,

and a hut

3. How did Buff find the bugs?

He rolled down a hill and hit a rock.

4. What did Buff do after he ate the bugs?

Buff curled up and took a nap.

Harcourt Brace School Publishers

Circle the word that names each picture. Then write the word.

1
limb
(lamb)
lame

lamb

2
pun
pan
(pen)

pen

3
(doll)
dull
dill

doll

4
trick
track
(truck)

truck

5
pine
(pin)
pain

pin

6
dune
dock
(double)

double

7
bad
bud
(bed)

bed

8
(tack)
tick
take

tack

9
hat
(hot)
hit

hot

10
pot
pat
(pet)

pet

11
fine
(fin)
fan

fin

12
(tub)
tube
tail

tub

SUPER REVIEW

Circle the letter or letters that stand for the short vowel sound in each picture name. Then write the letter or letters that complete the word.

1	2	3
i / u / (ou)	e / u / (a)	o / u / (e)
p__i__g	c__a__t	b__e__lt

4	5	6
a / (ou) / e	(o) / u / e	u / o / (e)
c__ou__ntry	r__o__ck	l__e__g

7	8	9
(u) / e / i	e / (a) / i	u / o / (i)
r__u__g	h__a__m	m__i__tt

10	11	12
(u) / a / e	u / a / (i)	e / (o) / a
c__u__b	p__i__n	m__o__p

Harcourt Brace School Publishers

Name _____

Fill in the circle next to the word that names the picture.

1
○ bat
○ bait
○ beat

2
○ tip
○ top
○ tap

3
○ hall
○ hike
○ hill

4
○ busy
○ bus
○ best

5
○ clock
○ cute
○ country

6
○ check
○ chick
○ cheek

7
○ sack
○ sock
○ soak

8
○ pan
○ pine
○ pen

9
○ rock
○ rake
○ road

10
○ dark
○ duke
○ duck

11
○ itch
○ ox
○ ax

12
○ kite
○ kit
○ cot

13
○ bag
○ big
○ bug

14
○ tub
○ tube
○ tab

15
○ mat
○ mitt
○ met

Fill in the circle next to the word that completes each sentence. Then write the word.

1. I like to _____run_____.	○ ruler ◉ run ○ rope
2. I can go very _____fast_____.	◉ fast ○ feast ○ face
3. I have a big _____dog_____.	○ dug ◉ dog ○ dig
4. He is _____black_____ with white spots.	○ bait ○ blame ◉ black
5. My dog likes to run _____with_____ me.	○ wide ○ when ◉ with
6. Sometimes he stops to _____dig_____.	◉ dig ○ dune ○ dime
7. I also have a _____young_____ cat.	○ yet ○ you ◉ young

Harcourt Brace School Publishers

feather

The word *feather* has the short *e* sound.
Write *ea* to complete each picture name that has
the short *e* sound.

1. tr ea sure

2. lamb l ___ mb

3. car c ___ r

4. br ea d

5. fox f ___ x

6. sw ea ter

7. rug r ___ g

8. w ea ther

9. van v ___ n

10. br ea kfast

11. mitt m ___ tt

12. thr ea d

13. bus b ___ s

14. duck d ___ ck

15. h ea d

Short Vowel: /e/*ea*   59

Name _____

Write the word that completes each sentence. You will not use all the words.

| feathers | breakfast | bird | meadow | sweater | read |
| heavy | spread | grass | bread | weather | ready |

1. Kate woke up and ate _____ breakfast _____.

2. The _____ weather _____ outside was sunny but cool.

3. Kate wore a _____ sweater _____ to keep her warm.

4. "Are you _____ ready _____?" Kate asked her friend Nancy.

5. The big picnic basket was _____ heavy _____!

6. The girls walked to a grassy _____ meadow _____.

7. They _____ spread _____ a blanket on the ground.

8. "Look at the bright _____ feathers _____ on that bird!" said Kate.

9. Kate and Nancy left crumbs of _____ bread _____ for the bird.

10. After they ate their lunch, the girls _____ read _____ a book.

Harcourt Brace School Publishers

The word *rain* has the long *a* sound. If a one-syllable word has two vowels, the first vowel is usually long and the second is usually silent. Write *ai* to complete each picture name that has the long *a* sound.

rain

1  sn__ai__l	2  ch__ai__n	3  flag fl_____g
4 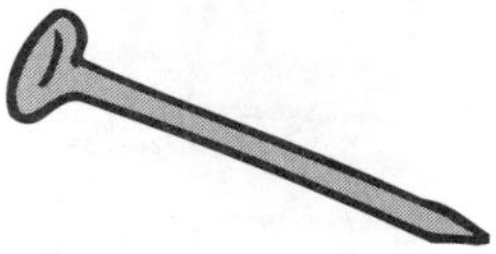 n__ai__l	5  mop m_____p	6  tr__ai__n
7  bed b_____d	8  br__ai__d	9  crib cr_____b
10  p__ai__nt	11  duck d_____ck	12  m__ai__l
13  cat c_____t	14  r__ai__n	15  t__ai__l

Long Vowel *a*

61

The letters *ay* can stand for the long *a* sound.
Write *ay* to complete each picture name that has
the long *a* sound.

jay

1	2	3
h__ay__	tr__ay__	toe t_____
4	5	6
pl__ay__	key k_____	d__ay__
7	8	9
p__ay__	cl__ay__	two t_____
10	11	12
gr__ay__	spr__ay__	pie p_____
13	14	15
st__ay__	tree tr_____	stingr__ay__

Phonics Practice Book

The word *skate* has the long *a* sound. If a one-syllable word has two vowels, the first vowel is usually long and the second is usually silent.
Write *a* and *e* to complete each picture name that has the long *a* sound.

sk<u>a</u>t<u>e</u>

1. wh a l e	2. w __ g	3. r a k e
4. c __ n	5. c a n e	6. c a v e
7. l a k e	8. c __ p	9. g a m e
10. c a k e	11. p __ g	12. p a g e
13. sn a k e	14. t __ p	15. w a v e

Name _____

rain　　　　　**jay**　　　　　**skate**

Circle the word that names each picture. Then write the word.

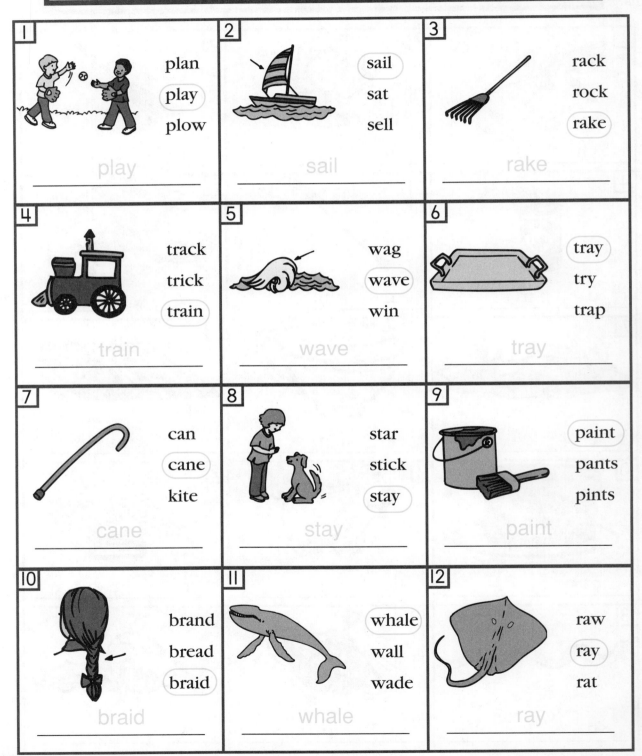

1	plan **play** plow	2	**sail** sat sell	3	rack rock **rake**

play　　　　　　sail　　　　　　rake

| 4 | track trick **train** | 5 | wag **wave** win | 6 | **tray** try trap |

train　　　　　　wave　　　　　　tray

| 7 | can **cane** kite | 8 | star stick **stay** | 9 | **paint** pants pints |

cane　　　　　　stay　　　　　　paint

| 10 | brand bread **braid** | 11 | **whale** wall wade | 12 | raw **ray** rat |

braid　　　　　　whale　　　　　　ray

Harcourt Brace School Publishers

Say the name of each picture. Circle the words in the box that rhyme with it.

1	skate	date	bait
		wait	mate
		scat	rat
		gate	sat
		plate	rate

2	snail	tale	pail
		fall	trail
		mail	sale
		tall	mat
		sill	ran

3	hay	way	may
		man	hill
		say	tray
		day	male
		hat	bay

4	train	try	pain
		rain	lane
		cane	brain
		trap	trim
		stain	man

5	rake	make	okay
		take	bake
		back	raid
		wake	fake
		rain	ray

Long Vowel *a*

Name _____

1. Jake likes to _____ skate _____ around the lake.

      scat   sat   (skate)

2. He wears roller _____ skates _____, a helmet, and pads.

      scats   (skates)   scours

3. Pads keep him from getting _____ scrapes _____ on his knees and elbows.

      (scrapes)   scraps   spoils

4. He just seems to _____ sail _____ past the people walking.

      (sail)   sack   sill

5. He zooms past the _____ mail _____ carrier.

      (mail)   mall   mill

6. As he goes by, he smiles and gives a big _____ wave _____.

      (wave)   wig   what

7. Jake skates every _____ day _____.

      dale   (day)   dot

8. Even a hard, cold _____ rain _____ does not stop him.

      ran   (rain)   red

9. Someday Jake may win a _____ race _____.

      risk   rack   (race)

10. His friend Ray _____ waits _____ for him at the end of the trail.

      (waits)   walls   wish

11. They like to _____ play _____ together at a nearby park.

      past   plow   (play)

12. After they play, the boys like to lie in the _____ shade _____ of a big tree.

      shack   (shade)   sad

Harcourt Brace School Publishers

Name _____

The words in the box are hidden in the puzzle. Some words go
down. Some words go across. Find and circle each one.

page	snail		
skate	clay		
whale	paint		
jay	train		
tray	play		

U	T	R	A	Y	C	X	P
X	R	Y	I	W	L	S	A
J	A	Y	T	H	A	K	I
I	I	P	L	A	Y	A	N
S	N	A	I	L	Z	T	T
L	P	A	G	E	K	E	R

Write the word from the puzzle that names each picture.

1	clay	2	skate
3	jay	**4**	snail
5	page	**6**	train
7	paint	**8**	tray
9	play	**10**	whale

Name _____

1. It is the long hair on a lion's head. _____

   man   may   (mane)

2. You can put flowers in it. _____

   vast   (vase)   vane

3. It is not night. _____

   (day)   dear   dare

4. You may ride in it on a trip. _____

   (train)   tray   trap

5. Cows like to eat this. _____

   ha   (hay)   heat

6. It's where you put your food. _____

   (plate)   plain   pat

7. It is a place to swim and sail. _____

   lack   lap   (lake)

8. It is what you do when you talk. _____

   save   (say)   sat

9. It is a place to keep a picture. _____

   (frame)   farm   fan

10. It is a way to say hello. _____

    (wave)   wall   wad

11. It is a blue bird. _____

    jail   lap   (jay)

Circle the sentence that best tells about the picture.

1		Will Dad and Jane bake a cake? (What can Dad and Jane make?) Did Jane go out to play?
2		Dad opens the mail. Dad gets a tray. (Dad has some nails.)
3		Jane gets out some hay. (Jane takes out wood scraps.) Jane plays with a toy train.
4		("This is the way to make it," Dad says.) "This is the way to play a horn," Dad says. "This is a very good cake," Dad says.
5		Jane waves to Dad. Jane puts it on a plate. (Jane paints it.)
6		(They will place it by the trail.) They will sail it on the lake. They will stay inside all day.

Name _____

The letters *ei* and *eigh* can stand for the long *a* sound. Circle the word that names the picture. Then write the word.

1	slit	2	reindeer	3	rests
	(sleigh)		record		rings
	sell		riddle		(reins)
	sleigh		reindeer		reins

4	neighbor	5	want	6	egg
	(neighbor)		(weight)		art
	nobody		wet		(eight)
	never				
	neighbor		weight		eight

Write a word from above to complete each sentence.

7. My next-door _____neighbor_____ has an odd pet.

8. It is a _____reindeer_____ with antlers.

9. He has had it for _____eight_____ years.

10. It can pull a lot of _____weight_____.

11. It can even pull a _____sleigh_____ over the snow.

12. Sometimes I get to hold the _____reins_____.

Harcourt Brace School Publishers

Name _____

The letters *ea* can stand for the long *a* sound. Write the word that answers each clue. You will not use all of the words.

break

braid	May	page	snail	tray
break	great	paint	steak	wave
hay	neighbor	play	train	whale

1. When you drop a glass, it may do this. _____ break

2. You can do this on a piano or with a game. _____ play

3. It is a small, slow animal that lives in a shell. _____ snail

4. This is part of a book. _____ page

5. It is something you use to make pictures. _____ paint

6. If something is really good, we call it this. _____ great

7. You can carry food on this. It is larger than a plate. _____ tray

8. This is someone who lives near your home. _____ neighbor

9. It is something that many people can ride in. It runs on a track.

_____ train

10. It is a kind of dried grass that a horse likes to eat. _____ hay

11. It is not a fish, but it looks like a big one. It is a huge sea animal.

_____ whale

12. It is something to eat. You can cook it on a grill. _____ steak

Name _____

Write each word under the correct heading.

baby	crayon	neighbor	plate	snake
baker	lady	weight	reindeer	stingray
clay	mayor	paint	snail	whale

People	Animals	Things
baby	reindeer	clay
_____	_____	_____
baker	snail	crayon
_____	_____	_____
lady	snake	weight
_____	_____	_____
mayor	stingray	paint
_____	_____	_____
neighbor	whale	plate
_____	_____	_____

Harcourt Brace School Publishers

Long Vowel: *a* • Sorting Words with Long *a*

The letters *ee* in *heel* stand for the long *e* sound. If a one-syllable word has two vowels, the first vowel is usually long and the second is usually silent. Write *ee* to complete each picture name that has the long *e* sound.

h__ee__l

1 wh__ee__l	2 f__ee__t	3 tr_____
4 w__ee__k	5 kn__ee__	6 s__ee__ds
7 t__ee__th	8 tr__ee__	9 sh__ee__p
10 sl__ee__p	11 s_____l	12 qu__ee__n
13 str__ee__t	14 n_____t	15 b__ee__

Harcourt Brace School Publishers

The letters *ea* can stand for the long *e* sound. If a one-syllable word has two vowels, the first vowel is usually long and the second is usually silent. Write *ea* to complete each picture name that has the long *e* sound.

st<u>ea</u>m

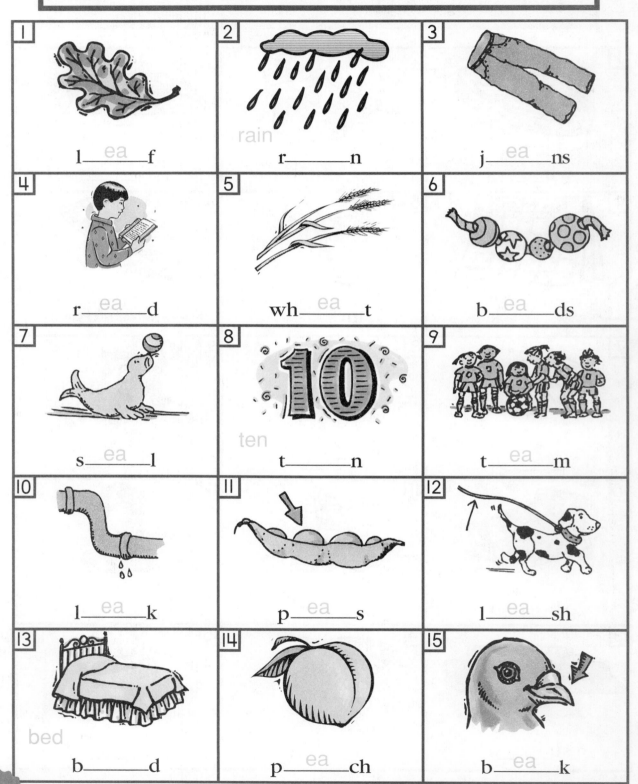

1	2	3
l__ea__f	rain r_____n	j__ea__ns
4	5	6
r__ea__d	wh__ea__t	b__ea__ds
7	8	9
s__ea__l	ten t_____n	t__ea__m
10	11	12
l__ea__k	p__ea__s	l__ea__sh
13	14	15
bed b_____d	p__ea__ch	b__ea__k

When *y* is at the end of a two-syllable word, it usually stands for the long *e* sound. Write *y* to complete each picture name that ends with the long *e* sound.

pupp_y_

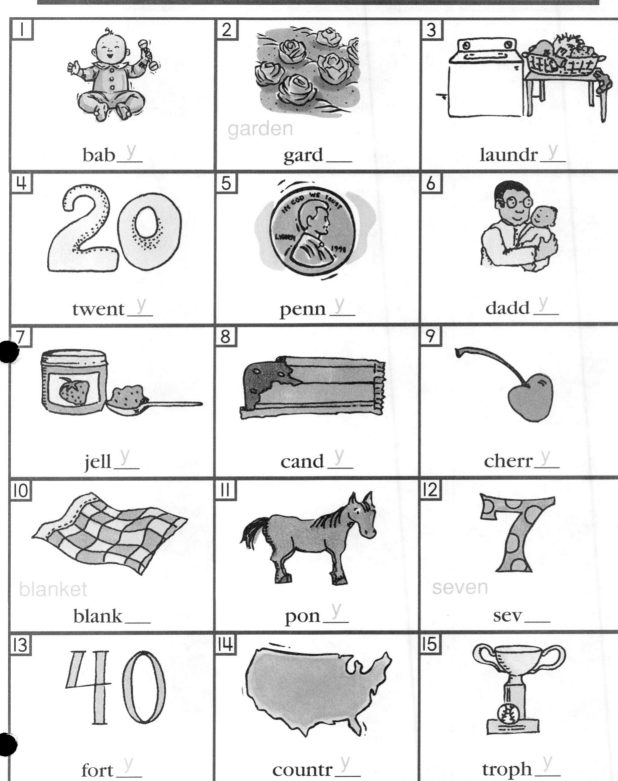

1 bab_y_	2 garden — gard___	3 laundr_y_
4 twent_y_	5 penn_y_	6 dadd_y_
7 jell_y_	8 cand_y_	9 cherr_y_
10 blanket — blank___	11 pon_y_	12 seven — sev___
13 fort_y_	14 countr_y_	15 troph_y_

When the letters *ey* are at the end of a two-syllable word, they usually stand for the long *e* sound. Write *ey* to complete each picture name that ends with the long *e* sound.

monkey

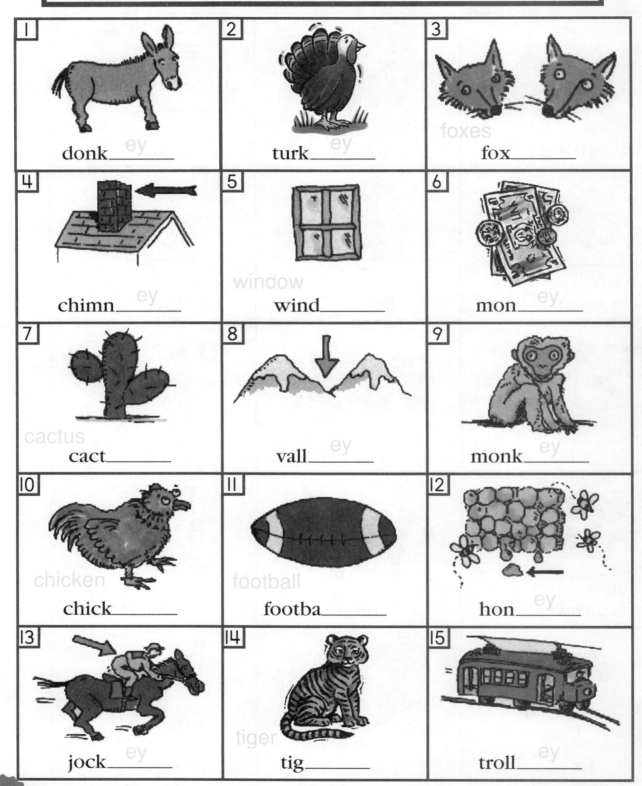

1	2	3
donk__ey__	turk__ey__	fox____
4	**5**	**6**
chimn__ey__	wind____	mon__ey__
7	**8**	**9**
cact____	vall__ey__	monk__ey__
10	**11**	**12**
chick____	footba____	hon__ey__
13	**14**	**15**
jock__ey__	tig____	troll__ey__

h<u>ee</u>l   st<u>ea</u>m   pupp<u>y</u>   mone<u>y</u>

Circle the name of each picture. Then write the word.

1	monkey · money · many	2	cane · keen · queen	3	count · country · cabin
4	jets · jacks · jeans	5	loaf · leaf · left	6	pony · pay · pine
7	many · money · motel	8	tea · try · tree	9	chimney · cheery · candy
10	wake · wreck · week	11	read · rod · red	12	beach · baby · barn
13	laundry · land · lady	14	whale · wheel · will	15	beds · bad · beads

1. monkey — circled: monkey — written: monkey
2. queen — circled: queen — written: queen
3. country — circled: country — written: country
4. jeans — circled: jeans — written: jeans
5. leaf — circled: leaf — written: leaf
6. pony — circled: pony — written: pony
7. money — circled: money — written: money
8. tree — circled: tree — written: tree
9. chimney — circled: chimney — written: chimney
10. week — circled: week — written: week
11. read — circled: read — written: read
12. baby — circled: baby — written: baby
13. laundry — circled: laundry — written: laundry
14. wheel — circled: wheel — written: wheel
15. beads — circled: beads — written: beads

Say the name of each picture. Circle the words that rhyme with it.

1	money	(funny) (try) (sunny) (honey) tree	(runny) cry (bunny) stay clay
2	tree	say (fee) (bee) (tea) (Lee)	dry (knee) (pea) (see) give
3	sheep	shop pay (deep) (leap) (weep)	(pep) (creep) (beep) (heap) pie
4	trolley	(holly) hello (Polly) (dolly) pal	golden (volley) (folly) trail (jolly)
5	seal	(feel) (deal) mall heat (meal)	(peel) (real) mail (squeal) (wheel)

Long Vowel: /ē/ee, ea, ie, y, ey

Phonics Practice Book

Harcourt Brace School Publishers

Name _____

Circle the word that best completes the sentence. Then write the word.

---

1. If you get a _____ , you must train it and care for it.

   (puppy)   pipe   padlock

2. You have to _____ it every day.

   (feed)   foot   fever

3. You also have to give it water _____ day.

   ache   (each)   enter

4. You need to brush the puppy and protect it from _____ .

   flaps   (fleas)   flutes

5. You _____ to be kind and loving to the puppy.

   next   not   (need)

6. Training a puppy is never _____ .

   eating   (easy)   eggs

7. You should _____ to it in a soft voice.

   (speak)   spark   speck

8. You should take it for a walk after each _____ .

   men   mail   (meal)

9. The puppy will have to get used to wearing its _____ .

   lash   leak   (leash)

Choose the word that fits each clue. Write the words in the puzzle.

cheek   knee   street
chimney   party   tea
eat   please   teeth
happy   read   turkey
sea

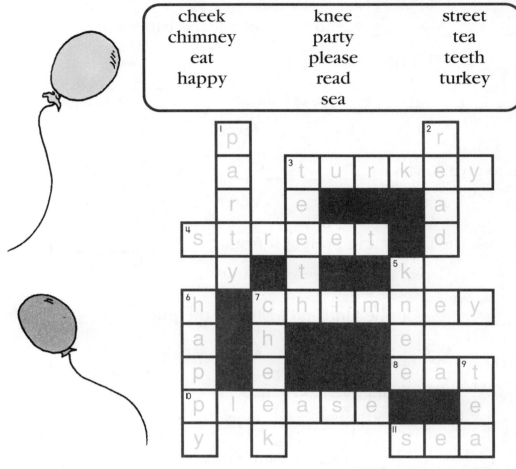

ACROSS

3. A Thanksgiving bird

4. A place where people drive cars

7. Smoke comes out of this

8. What you do at a meal

10. A polite word

11. A large body of water

DOWN

1. A fun gathering of friends

2. What you do with a book

3. What you need to brush often

5. The joint in the middle of your leg

6. The opposite of *sad*

7. A part of your face

9. Something to drink

Long Vowel *e* • Reading Words with Long *e*

Harcourt Brace School Publishers

Phonics Practice Book

Circle the word that fits each clue. Then write the word.

1. This is what we do with food. _____eat_____

   yet   end   (eat)

2. This fruit makes a juicy snack. ____peach____

   pest   (peach)   please

3. The bread we eat is made from this grain. ____wheat____

   whale   (wheat)   wet

4. This small red fruit grows on trees. ____cherry____

   (cherry)   cheer   check

5. Many people grill or bake this food. ____meat____

   met   (meat)   marry

6. Some people eat this with stuffing and gravy. ____turkey____

   turtle   tunnel   (turkey)

7. Desserts taste this way. ____sweet____

   (sweet)   set   sleep

8. This is a treat you should not eat too often. ____candy____

   city   (candy)   chimney

9. You should floss these each day. ____teeth____

   teach   tell   (teeth)

10. It is fun to eat meals with them. ____family____

   feel   (family)   free

Circle the sentence that tells about the picture.

1		Leesa goes to the beach.
		(Leesa loves to read.)
		Leesa plants a seed.
2		She enjoys eating.
		(She enjoys any kind of story.)
		She enjoys seeing the monkey on TV.
3		(This book is a good fairy tale.)
		This is a big tree.
		This is a good meal.
4		It is about a queen who has a monkey.
		It is about a turkey who loves candy.
		(It is about a donkey who turns into a prince.)
5		(Leesa sees herself in every story.)
		Leesa sees the baby in the crib.
		Leesa sees a sheep in the garden.
6		Today she walks her pet dog on a leash.
		Today she is wading in a stream.
		(Today she is the girl who made the team.)
7		Leesa leaps out of bed every morning.
		(Leesa reads every night before she goes to sleep.)
		Leesa sleeps with twenty teddy bears.
8		(Then she dreams about the story she just read.)
		Leesa never has a dream at night.
		Leesa dreams she is weeding the garden.

Long Vowel *e* • Reading Words in Context

Harcourt Brace School Publishers

The letters *ie* can stand for the long *e* sound.
Circle the word that names the picture.

coll<u>ie</u>

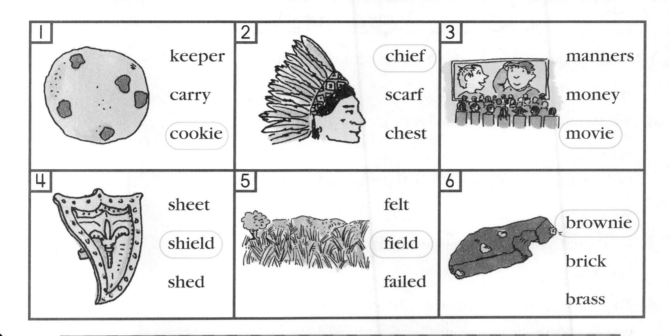

1		2		3	
	keeper		chief		manners
	carry		scarf		money
	(cookie)		chest		(movie)

4		5		6	
	sheet		felt		(brownie)
	(shield)		(field)		brick
	shed		failed		brass

Write the word from the box that best completes each sentence.

thief	believe	shriek	collie	rookie	relief

7. Ernie was a new player—the _____ rookie _____ on the team.

8. Ernie did not _____ believe _____ he could get a hit.

9. What a _____ relief _____ it was when he hit the ball!

10. Then Ernie heard a loud _____ shriek _____.

11. Someone screamed, "Stop, _____ thief _____!"

12. Ernie's dog, a _____ collie _____, had run off with the ball.

Name _____

Write the word that answers each clue. You will not use all the words.

> beak   donkey   knee   seal
> bee   easy   neat   sorry
> city   honey   peach   teeth

1. It is the name of a pinkish color or a juicy fruit.

   What is it? _____peach_____

2. We would not have this sweet treat without bees.

   What is it? _____honey_____

3. Does a bird have lips? No, it has this instead.

   What is it? _____beak_____

4. It is what you say when you hurt someone's feelings.

   What is it? _____sorry_____

5. You have these in your mouth and in your comb.

   What are they? _____teeth_____

6. It sounds like the name of a letter. It is also the name of an insect.

   What is it? _____bee_____

7. It is a busy place to live. It is bigger than a town.

   What is it? _____city_____

8. It is the opposite of *messy*.

   What is it? _____neat_____

9. It names a sea animal or tells
   what you do to an envelope.

   What is it? _____seal_____

10. Without one of these, your
    leg would not bend.

    What is it? _____knee_____

Long Vowel *e* • Reading Words with Long *e*

Phonics Practice Book

Write the word that names the picture.

> rein jay tree steak play feet
> field snail monkey seal wheel
> mail pea cookie train

1 monkey	2 snail	3 field
4 feet	5 play	6 steak
7 tree	8 jay	9 rein
10 seal	11 train	12 cookie
13 mail	14 wheel	15 pea

Name _____

A Morning Sail

Lee goes out in his sailboat
At the very break of day.
Lee lives right down beside the beach.
He starts each day this way.

Lee waves to all the neighbors
He sees along the way—
To fishers with their pails of bait
And farmers raking hay.

The journey is a brief one.
He pulls into the bay.
But Lee is always happy
When he starts his day this way.

Possible responses are shown.

1. Where does Lee live?

   right down beside the beach

2. What does Lee go out in?

   his sailboat

3. Who does Lee see each day?

   the neighbors he sees along the way, fishers, farmers

If a one-syllable word has two vowels, the first vowel is usually long and the second is usually silent. Write *i* and *e* to complete each picture name that has the long *i* sound.

kite

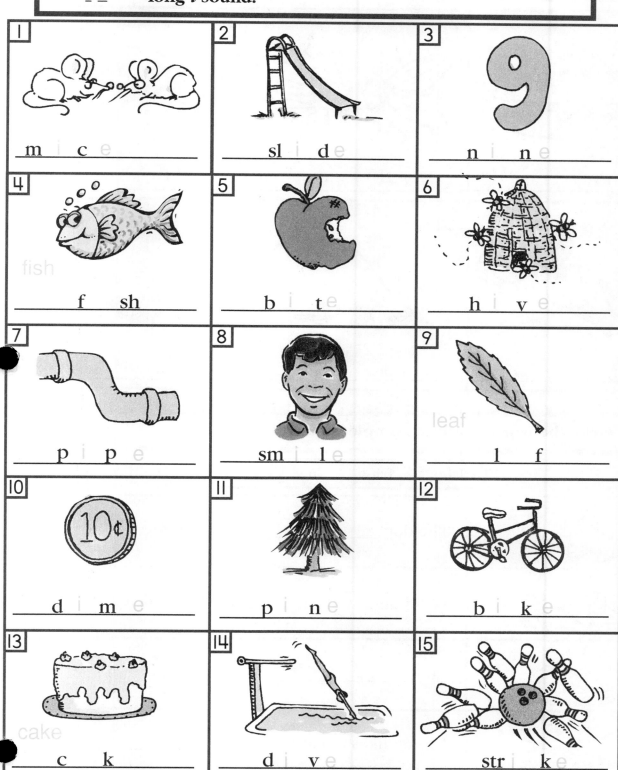

1	2	3
m i c e	sl i d e	n i n e
4	5	6
f i sh	b i t e	h i v e
7	8	9
p i p e	sm i l e	l i f
10	11	12
d i m e	p i n e	b i k e
13	14	15
c k	d i v e	str i k e

Harcourt Brace School Publishers

The letters *ie* can stand for the long *i* sound.
Write *ie* to complete each picture name that has the long *i* sound.

t**ie**

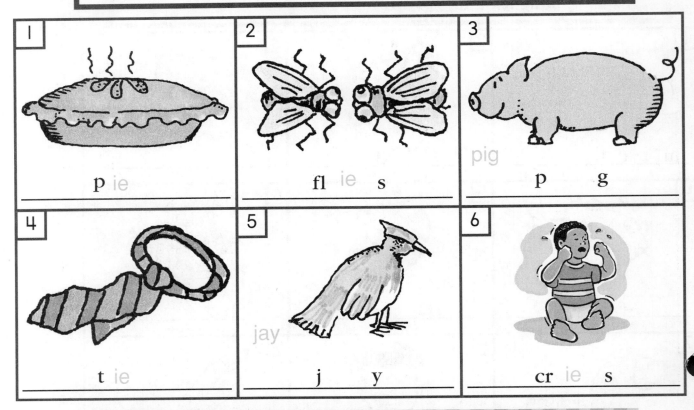

1. p **ie**

2. fl **ie** s

3. pig

   p _ g

4. t **ie**

5. jay

   j _ y

6. cr **ie** s

Write the word that best completes each sentence.

dries   fries   lies   tries

7. The dog _____lies_____ by the fire.

8. Cindy _____tries_____ to win the race.

9. Sam _____dries_____ the dishes.

10. Lauren likes to eat french _____fries_____.

Harcourt Brace School Publishers

Phonics Practice Book

The letters *igh* stand for the long *i* sound. Fill in the letters *igh* when the picture name has the long *i* sound.

light

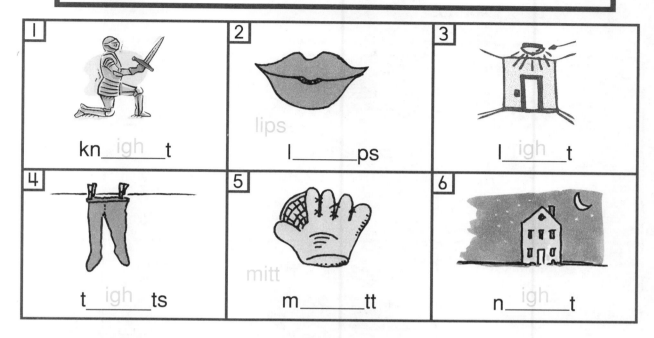

1. kn__igh__t

2. l_____ps

3. l__igh__t

4. t__igh__ts

5. m_____tt

6. n__igh__t

Write the word that best completes each sentence. You will not use all the words.

(right   bite   bright   fright   flight   bridge)

7. The driver turned on her _____ bright _____ lights to see the road better.

8. Juan takes a late-night _____ flight _____ to visit his grandmother.

9. The officer tells Jay to turn _____ right _____ at the next traffic light.

Harcourt Brace School Publishers

When *y* is at the end of a one-syllable word, it usually stands for the long *i* sound. Write *y* to complete each picture name that ends with the long *i* sound.

dry

1	2	3
fl__y__	sea s____	sk__y__

4	5	6
cr__y__	tree tr____	dr__y__

7	8	9
play pl____	tray tr____	jay j____

10	11	12
fr__y__	say s____	sh__y__

k<u>i</u>te   **t<u>ie</u>**   **l<u>igh</u>t**   **dr<u>y</u>**

Circle the word that names each picture. Then write the word.

1	pea	2	slid	3	stay
	(pie)		sleep		skip
	pay		(slide)		(sky)
	pie		slide		sky

4	(high)	5	miss	6	dim
	hip		(mice)		dream
	hay		mike		(dime)
	high		mice		dime

7	tea	8	(knight)	9	flees
	tame		knee		(flies)
	(tie)		knit		fleas
	tie		knight		flies

10	(pine)	11	strips	12	dress
	pin		straps		(dries)
	pain		(stripes)		dream
	pine		stripes		dries

13	frees	14	(bite)	15	fray
	(fries)		bit		free
	frays		bait		(fry)
	fries		bite		fry

Read the poem, and think about what happens.

Hide and Go Seek

It's hide-and-go-seek time.
Let's get out of sight.
This time they won't find us
If they hunt all night!

I'll lie on the branch of
This nice old tree,
And you hide behind it
As still as can be.

I wish we could fly
High up in the sky
Where they couldn't find us.
They'd never guess why!

Write the answers to the questions.

Possible responses are shown.

1. What game does the poem tell about?

    hide-and-go-seek

2. What does the speaker have to do?

    get out of sight, hide

3. Where does the speaker hide?

    on the branch of an old tree

4. Where does the speaker wish they could hide?

    high up in the sky

Write the word that best completes the sentence.

midnight	quite	beside	try	tried	my	fright
smile	light	dine	right	time	outside	flashlight

1. The clock struck _____ midnight _____.

2. Mike heard a crash _____ beside/outside _____ the house.

3. Mike _____ tried _____ to hide under the covers.

4. He shook with _____ fright _____.

5. Then Dad turned on the _____ light _____.

6. "Are you all _____ right _____?" asked Dad.

7. "Do you know what is _____ outside _____?" Mike asked.

8. Dad had a _____ flashlight _____ in his hand.

9. Mike was not _____ quite _____ sure that they should go see.

10. He decided to _____ try _____ to be brave.

11. "Oh _____ my _____!" laughed Mike.

12. He gave a _____ smile _____ of delight.

13. Two raccoons had come to _____ dine _____.

14. They were having a great _____ time _____!

Harcourt Brace School Publishers

The words below are in the puzzle. Some words go down, and some words go across. Find and circle each one.

bike	cries	flies	knight	light
pie	pine	sky	side	smile

X P I N E S K Y
L I G H T Y R X
Y E F L I E S B
K N I G H T X I
S M I L E Z Y K
C R I E S I D E

Write the word from the puzzle that names each picture.

1. light

2. sky

3. bike

4. pie

5. knight

6. smile

7. flies

8. cries

Harcourt Brace School Publishers

Phonics Practice Book

Write the word that fits each clue. You will not use all of the words.

| why | bike | mile | light | fright | slide |
| bright | sight | lie | size | tie | fly | pie | file |

1. It is something to ride that has only two wheels.

   _____

2. It means "not heavy" or "not dark." _____

3. It is fun to bake and good to eat. _____

4. It is a scared feeling. _____

5. This is a long way to walk. _____

6. This word often begins a question. _____

7. You can wear one of these or do it to your shoelaces.

   _____

8. It is one of your five senses. _____

9. It is the opposite of *truth*. _____

10. It is something both a bird and an airplane can do. _____

11. It can be small, medium, or large. _____

12. It is something you might see in a park or what you do into

    home plate. _____

Harcourt Brace School Publishers

Circle the sentence that tells about the picture.

1. "Here is a kite," said Mama Bird.
"Go to sleep. It is night," said Mama Bird.
(It is time to fly," said Mama Bird.)

2. Baby Bird had a bite to eat.
(Baby Bird looked up at the sky.)
Baby Bird went down the slide.

3. "I will need a flashlight up there," she said.
"I will ride a bike up there," she said.
("I will have a fine time up there," she said.)

4. (Then Baby Bird looked down from the pine.)
Then Baby Bird fried leaves in a pan.
Then Baby Bird went on a hayride.

5. Baby Bird slid down the vine.
(Baby Bird was filled with fright.)
Baby Bird cheeped with delight.

6. ("No!" cried Baby Bird. "It is too high.")
"Yes!" cried Baby Bird. "I would love some pie."
"Oh, dear!" cried Baby Bird. "I need a new tie."

7. Rain began falling from the sky.
Baby Bird could not fly.
(Baby Bird could fly!)

8. Now Baby Bird rides on the train.
(Now Baby Bird flies all the time.)
Now Baby Bird sits in the pine.

Name _____

When the letter *i* is followed by *nd, ld,* or *gn,* it often stands for the long *i* sound.

beh<u>ind</u>   chi<u>ld</u>   si<u>gn</u>

Write the word that answers each question.

behind   bind   child   find   kind
mind   blinds   rind   sign   wild   wind

1. Which word is the opposite of *lose*? _____ *find*

2. Which word names what you use to think? _____ *mind*

3. Which word tells what you do when you write your name? _____ *sign*

4. Which word is the opposite of *tame*? _____ *wild*

5. Which word means "to tie with string"? _____ *bind*

6. Which word names something that covers a window? _____ *blinds*

7. Which word is the opposite of *in front of*? _____ *behind*

8. Which word can name the skin of a fruit? _____ *rind*

9. Which word tells what you do to keep some clocks running? _____ *wind*

10. Which word is the opposite of *mean*? _____ *kind*

11. Which word names a person who is still very young? _____ *child*

Look at the picture. Then follow the directions.

1.   Draw window blinds on one window.
     window blinds are drawn on one window

2.   On the other window write *Pop's Diner.*
     Pop's Diner is written on the other window

3.   Write *Try* it! at the bottom of the sign.
     Try it! is written on the bottom of the sign

4.   Circle the frying pans on the wall.
     frying pans on the wall are circled

5.   Mark an X on the diner's tie.
     diner's tie is marked with an X

6.   Draw a glass of milk beside the slice of pie.
     glass of milk is drawn beside the pie

7.   Draw a table knife in the boy's hand.
     table knife is drawn in the boy's hand

8.   Add a napkin beside the child's plate.
     napkin is drawn beside the boy's plate

Now circle all the long *i* words in the directions.

The word *soap* has the long *o* sound. If a one-syllable word has two vowels, the first vowel is usually long and the second is usually silent. Write *oa* to complete each picture name that has the long *o* sound.

s**oa**p

1. c_**oa**_t	2. d___g	3. b_**oa**_t
4. c___t	5. l_**oa**_f	6. r_**oa**_d
7. c_**oa**_l	8. s___l	9. g_**oa**_t
10. fl_**oa**_t	11. f___t	12. t_**oa**_st
13. t_**oa**_d	14. h___t	15. c_**oa**_ch

The word *rose* has the long *o* sound.
Write *o* and *e* to complete each picture name that has the long *o* sound.

r**o**se

1. c **o** n **e**	2. n **o** s **e**	3. n **o** t **e**
4. r **o** p **e**	5. p __ t	6. ph **o** n **e**
7. h **o** s **e**	8. sm **o** k **e**	9. sl __ d
10. r **o** b **e**	11. st **o** v **e**	12. b **o** n **e**
13. sn __ k	14. t __ p	15. gl **o** b **e**

The letters *ow* can stand for the long *o* sound.
Write *ow* to complete each picture name that has
the long *o* sound.

crow

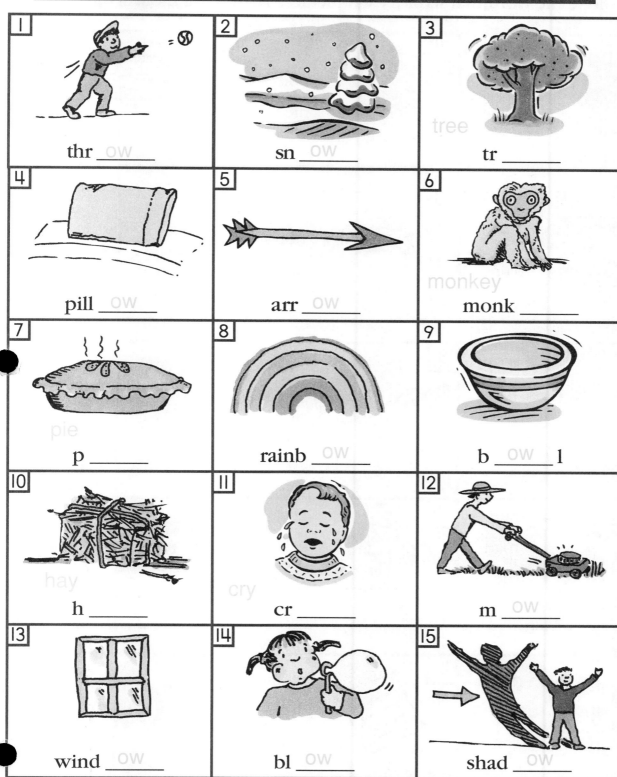

1	2	3
thr __ow__	sn __ow__	tr _____

4	5	6
pill __ow__	arr __ow__	monk _____

7	8	9
p _____	rainb __ow__	b __ow__ l

10	11	12
h _____	cr _____	m __ow__

13	14	15
wind __ow__	bl __ow__	shad __ow__

Name_____

 soap    **rose**   **crow**

Circle the word that names each picture. Then write the word.

1	coat	cot	crate	coat
2	nose	nod	nice	nose
3	bait	box	boat	boat

4	phone	pond	pain	phone
5	raining	ribbon	rainbow	rainbow
6	snail	snow	sob	snow

7	arrow	arm	armor	arrow
8	rope	rod	ripe	rope
9	glad	glob	globe	globe

10	rate	road	rod	road
11	cost	cash	coach	coach
12	tied	toad	top	toad

13	tow	tea	ton	tow
14	night	not	note	note
15	shopping	shadow	shading	shadow

Name _____

Load up the big semi,
Then start up and go.
This rig can't be stopped
By rain or by snow.

One goal has the driver,
Who lives on the road—
Get the goods there on time,
Then quickly unload.

Pick up a new load
In the loading zone,
Then back on the road again—
Always alone.

Possible responses are shown.

1. What must the driver of a big rig do before setting out?

   load up the semi
   _____

2. What cannot stop this driver's rig?

   rain or snow
   _____

3. What is every truck driver's goal?

   get the goods there on time and then unload quickly
   _____

4. Where does the driver pick up a new load?

   in the loading zone
   _____

5. What would be a good title for the poem?

   Responses will vary.
   _____

Now underline the long *o* words in the poem.

Name _____

Circle the word that best completes the sentence. Then write the word.

1. The _____crows_____ ate Farmer Rose's corn.
   cots   crates   (crows)

2. Farmer Rose went _____home_____ very angry.
   (home)   him   honey

3. "I will _____show_____ them," he said.
   sob   (show)   say

4. "I will make a _____scarecrow_____."
   (scarecrow)   saddle   soccer

5. At home, Mrs. Rose was on the _____phone_____ .
   fog   (phone)   fun

6. She did not _____know_____ what Farmer Rose was up to.
   cob   cake   (know)

7. Farmer Rose got Mrs. Rose's _____robe_____ .
   rob   read   (robe)

8. He got a _____bowl_____ for a hat.
   bill   (bowl)   bond

9. He needed a _____pole_____ to finish the scarecrow.
   (pole)   pond   par

10. That night Mrs. Rose looked high and _____low_____ for her robe.
    lie   (low)   lot

11. Then she looked out the _____window_____ .
    (window)   wife   wall

12. "Oh, no," _____groaned_____ Mrs. Rose.
    grain   got   (groaned)

13. "You should have _____known_____ I would need my robe."
    kind   (known)   kid

14. "Well," said Farmer Rose, "may I use your _____coat_____ instead?"
    kite   cat   (coat)

Long Vowel *o* • Reading Words with Long *o*

Phonics Practice Book

Harcourt Brace School Publishers

Name _____

Write the word in the puzzle that fits each clue.

coach   coal   doze   drove   hole   home   phone
pillow   rainbow   road   shadow   soap   window

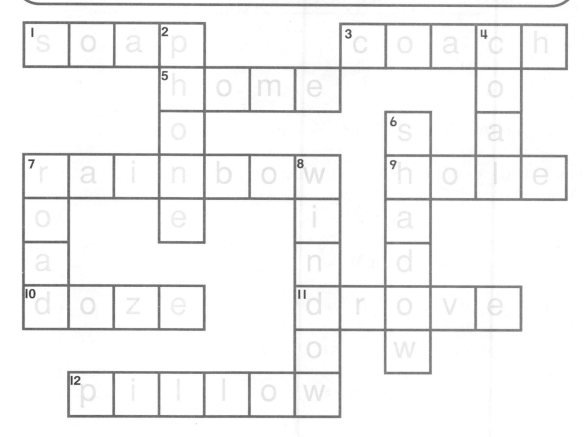

Across
1. You wash your hands with it.
3. The teacher of a sports team
5. People live here.
7. Bright colors in the sky
9. Something you can dig
10. To take a short nap
11. What Mom did with the car
12. A soft place for your head

Down
2. What you use to call people
4. People get it from a mine.
6. It follows you on a sunny day.
7. A place to drive a car
8. Something to look out of

Write the word that fits each clue.

foal	rope	hole	slow	globe
low	mow	phone	oats	throne
float	woke	croak	roast	joke

1. You tell one to make people laugh.   _joke_ _____

2. You can tie things up with this.   _rope_ _____

3. When it rings, you pick it up.   _phone_ _____

4. It is the sound a frog makes.   _croak_ _____

5. You do this to food in your oven.   _roast_ _____

6. This is something you can do in the water.   _float_ _____

7. A horse thinks this is a treat.   _oats_ _____

8. It is a map in the shape of the Earth.   _globe_ _____

9. This is something you make when you dig.   _hole_ _____

10. It is the opposite of *high*.   _low_ _____

11. It is a chair for a king or a queen.   _throne_ _____

12. It is the first thing you did this morning.   _woke_ _____

13. It is something you do to grass.   _mow_ _____

14. It is the opposite of *fast*.   _slow_ _____

15. It is a name for a baby horse.   _foal_ _____

Harcourt Brace School Publishers

Circle the sentence that tells about the picture.

1

(Joan and Mom load up the car.)

Joan and Mom get on their bikes.

Joan and Mom are on the phone.

2

They see a rainbow in the snow.

They float on their backs down the stream.

(They go to the cove by the lake.)

3

They like to stay home.

They eat ice-cream cones.

(They get into the boat.)

4

They phone home from the park.

(They row to the park.)

They run up the slope.

5

(Mom ties the boat with a rope.)

Mom floats away in the boat.

Joan likes to jump rope.

6

(It looks as if they are all alone.)

They put on their coats.

They look at the globe.

7

Mom broke the rope.

Mom cooks oats on the stove.

(Soon smoke will rise from the fire.)

8

They dig a hole.

(They roast hot dogs.)

They pick a rose.

O
zero

The letter *o* can stand for the long *o* sound.
Write the word that names the picture.

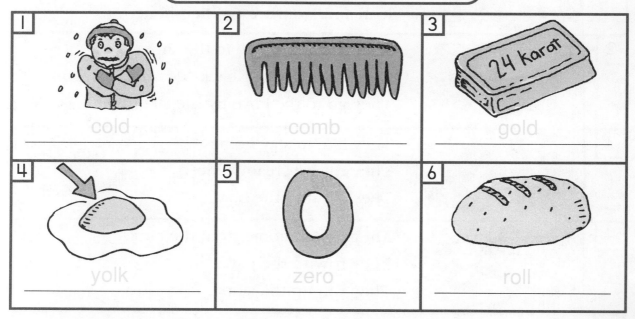

yolk   roll   cold   zero   gold   comb

1. cold

2. comb

3. gold

4. yolk

5. zero

6. roll

Write the word that best completes each sentence.

over   colt   fold   go   hold   old

7. This _____ old _____ game is still fun to play.

8. Draw a _____ colt _____ without a tail.

9. Then _____ fold _____ a big scarf to make
a blindfold.

10. Tie the blindfold _____ over _____ your eyes.

11. In your hand, _____ hold _____ the colt's tail.

12. Now _____ go _____ to the colt, and try
to pin the tail to the right spot.

Write the word that answers each clue.

bowl	elbow	note	rose
coat	grow	rainbow	show
code	hose	rope	slow

1. You can water a garden with it. _____hose_____

2. You can jump with it or tie something with it. _____rope_____

3. It is the name of a flower. _____rose_____

4. It means "not fast." _____slow_____

5. You wear one when it is cold outside. _____coat_____

6. If the sun shines through rain, you may see one of these.

   _____rainbow_____

7. It is a short letter or a part of a song. _____note_____

8. Your address has a ZIP _____code_____.

9. It is another name for a movie. _____show_____

10. It is something you eat cereal and other foods out of.

    _____bowl_____

11. A plant does it quickly. You do it too, but slowly. _____grow_____

12. You can bend your arm because you have this. _____elbow_____

Name _____

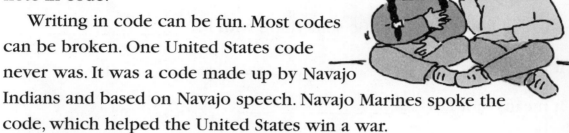

SECRET CODES

Would you like to write a note to a friend that no one else can read? Then write your note in code!

Writing in code can be fun. Most codes can be broken. One United States code never was. It was a code made up by Navajo Indians and based on Navajo speech. Navajo Marines spoke the code, which helped the United States win a war.

There are many ways to make up your own codes. You can write your note backward, like this: .eert kao eht ta em teeM.

You can also make up a number code. For an easy number code, use 1 for *A*, 2 for *B*, and so on. This code is shown below:

1=A	2=B	3=C	4=D	5=E	6=F	7=G	8=H
9=I	10=J	11=K	12=L	13=M	14=N	15=O
16=P	17=Q	18=R	19=S	20=T	21=U	22=V
23=W	24=X	25=Y	26=Z

Possible responses are shown.

1. Who made up a code that was never broken? ___Navajo Indians___

2. Decode this message:

   14 15 23 / 25 15 21 / 11 14 15 23 / 1 12 12 /

   1 2 15 21 20 / 12 15 14 7 / 15.

Now you know all about long o.

_____

_____

Harcourt Brace School Publishers

Circle the letter or letters that stand for the long vowel sound in the picture name. Then write the word.

REVIEW

1	i-e ai (oa)	2	ay (ie) oa	3	i-e a-e (o-e)
	coat _____		tie _____		bone _____

4	(i-e) ow ea	5	igh (o-e) ea	6	ea ai (oa)
	bike _____		rope _____		road _____

7	a-e (igh) oa	8	(ow) ie a-e	9	(y) ea o-e
	night _____		snow _____		fly _____

10	ie (ow) ea	11	ee ai (ie)	12	oa a-e (igh)
	mow _____		flies _____		light _____

13	o i-e ai	14	ee (i-e) ai	15	(ie) ay ea
	cold _____		dive _____		pie _____

Review of Long Vowels *i* and *o*

113

Name _____

REVIEW

Read the poem. Then write the answers to the questions.

Showtime at the Fair

Di will show her new colt.
Joan will show her pet goat.
Joe's fine golden duckling
Will dive and float.

Bo has baby chicks
That cannot fly high.
They hide behind Mother Hen,
Tiny and shy.

I ride a white pony
Just right for my size.
Oh, here come the judges—
Hope I win a prize!

Possible responses are shown.

1. What will Di and Joan show?

_____ a colt and a goat _____

2. What do the baby chicks do?

_____ hide behind the mother hen _____

3. What will the judges do?

_____ They will give out prizes. _____

4. What pet will the speaker of the poem show?

_____ A white pony just right for her size. _____

Name _____

The word *mule* has the long *u* sound.
Write the letters *u* and *e* to complete each picture name that has the long *u* sound.

mule

| 1 | 2 | 3 |
| t u b e | t _ b | t u n e |

tub

| 4 | 5 | 6 |
| fl u t e | r u l e r | th _ mb |

thumb

| 7 | 8 | 9 |
| c u b e | c _ b | n _ t |

cub   nut

| 10 | 11 | 12 |
| pr u n e | l _ mb | b _ g |

lamb   bug

| 13 | 14 | 15 |
| j _ mp | p _ ppy | J u n e |

jump   puppy

Harcourt Brace School Publishers

Name _____

Come march to our tune.
Bring your flute to play.
We're going to have
A parade today.

We'll wear uniforms
And hats with plumes,
While some twirl batons
In cute costumes.

Possible responses are shown.

1. What are the children going to do?

   march to the tune; bring a flute to play

2. What does the speaker invite a friend to do?

   join the parade

3. What would be a good title for the poem?

   Responses will vary.

Long Vowel: /(y)o͞o/u-e • Reading Words in Context

Phonics Practice Book

Harcourt Brace School Publishers

Circle the word that best completes the sentence. Then write the word.

1. Try not to be _____rude_____ .

   red   (rude)   run

2. Push toothpaste from the bottom of the _____tube_____ .

   tab   tub   (tube)

3. Don't _____refuse_____ to share.

   recall   reef   (refuse)

4. Don't _____pollute_____ the Earth with litter.

   (pollute)   pillow   polo

5. Be kind to animals, even _____mules_____ .

   miles   (mules)   mugs

6. Say thank you if someone says you're _____cute_____ .

   curl   (cute)   cutter

7. Try to follow the _____tune_____ when you sing.

   (tune)   ton   tulip

8. Chewing ice _____cubes_____ may break a tooth.

   canes   (cubes)   cubs

9. Throw your dirty clothes in the laundry _____chute_____ .

   shut   chain   (chute)

10. Keep the _____volume_____ down on your radio.

    valley   (volume)   very

11. Don't _____use_____ your brother's toys.

    (use)   as   us

12. Don't make too many _____rules_____ .

    (rules)   rolls   rails

The words below are in the puzzle. Some words go down. Some words go across. Find and circle each one.

chute   cube   dune   flute   June   mule
plume   pollute   tube   tune   cute

X	A	R	F	T	H	I	C
P	O	L	L	U	T	E	H
L	I	C	U	B	E	J	U
U	C	U	T	E	Z	U	T
M	U	L	E	T	U	N	E
E	Z	D	U	N	E	E	U

Write the word from the puzzle that names each picture. You will not use all of the words.

1. cube _____

2. flute _____

3. mule _____

4. tube _____

5. June _____

6. tune _____

Long Vowel: /(y)o͞o/u-e

Phonics Practice Book

Harcourt Brace School Publishers

Write the word that fits each clue.

tune	cube	parachute	June	mule	flute
plume	huge	costume	cute	spruce	pollute

1. It is an animal that is like a horse. _____mule_____

2. It is the opposite of tiny. _____huge_____

3. People play pretty music on this. _____flute_____

4. It is a month of the year. _____June_____

5. It is the feather on a hat. _____plume_____

6. It's what people say babies are. _____cute_____

7. Our planet will stay clean if we don't do this. _____pollute_____

8. You can play or sing this. _____tune_____

9. You may wear this if you act in a play. _____costume_____

10. It is a kind of tree. _____spruce_____

11. You'd better wear this if you jump out of a plane. _____parachute_____

12. It is a word for a square piece of ice. _____cube_____

Circle the sentence that tells about the picture.

1

In June, Luke went to a dude ranch.

In June, Luke had flute lessons.

In June, Luke slid down a dune.

2

Luke wore a mule costume.

Luke wore a grand duke costume.

Luke wore a cowhand outfit.

3

His job was to cut down a huge spruce.

His job was to feed the mules.

His job was to write the rules.

4

Luke used a flute for the first time.

Luke rode a huge horse for the first time.

Luke pruned a tree for the first time.

5

He petted a huge mule.

He petted a bird with a plumed tail.

He petted a cute baby calf.

6

The cowhands sang and played tunes.

The cowhands were rude.

The cowhands refused to smile.

Name _____

Circle the word that names each picture. Then write the word.

1	try / (tree) / tray	tree
2	(mule) / mile / meal	mule
3	(whale) / while / wheel	whale

4	sneak / snake / (snow)	snow
5	late / (light) / lute	light
6	(goat) / gate / greet	goat

7	tea / (tie) / tow	tie
8	mule / need / (nail)	nail
9	came / climb / (comb)	comb

10	sole / sail / (seal)	seal
11	true / (tray) / tree	tray
12	reap / ripe / (rope)	rope

13	(bike) / bake / beak	bike
14	flows / flees / (flies)	flies
15	crow / (cry) / creep	cry

Name _____

Circle the sentence that tells about the picture.

1. The whale slides down the chute.

   Whales like to ride in boats.

   (A whale is a huge animal.)

2. Look at the frisky colts.

   (Goats and mules graze at the farm.)

   Goats and mules sleep in the house.

3. (White mice make good pets.)

   The mice are eating ice cream.

   The white mice are running away.

4. (Most people do not like flies.)

   The plane is high up in the sky.

   Some people do not like to cry.

5. A wild bunny does not have a tail.

   A wild bunny likes to fly.

   (A wild bunny is often shy.)

6. The seal is on the beach.

   (Seals can do funny tricks.)

   The seal is in the seat.

7. (Bats like to fly at night.)

   Bats fly when it is light.

   A bat cannot fly.

8. The snail is in the pail.

   Cats have sharp nails.

   (Snails are very slow.)

Fill in the circle next to the word that names each picture.

1.
○ crack
● cry
○ crow

2.
○ scat
● skate
○ skirt

3.
● seal
○ sell
○ sale

4.
○ meal
○ mill
● mule

5.
○ cot
● coat
○ cute

6.
● monkey
○ milky
○ muddy

7.
○ bin
● bone
○ burn

8.
○ pint
○ pant
● paint

9.
● field
○ fold
○ fade

10.
○ pay
○ pea
● pie

11.
○ flat
● flute
○ float

12.
● hay
○ ha
○ hi

13.
○ cope
○ cap
● cape

14.
● knight
○ knee
○ knit

15.
○ pen
○ pillow
● penny

CHECK-UP

Fill in the circle next to the letters that stand for the long vowel sound in each picture name. Then write the word.

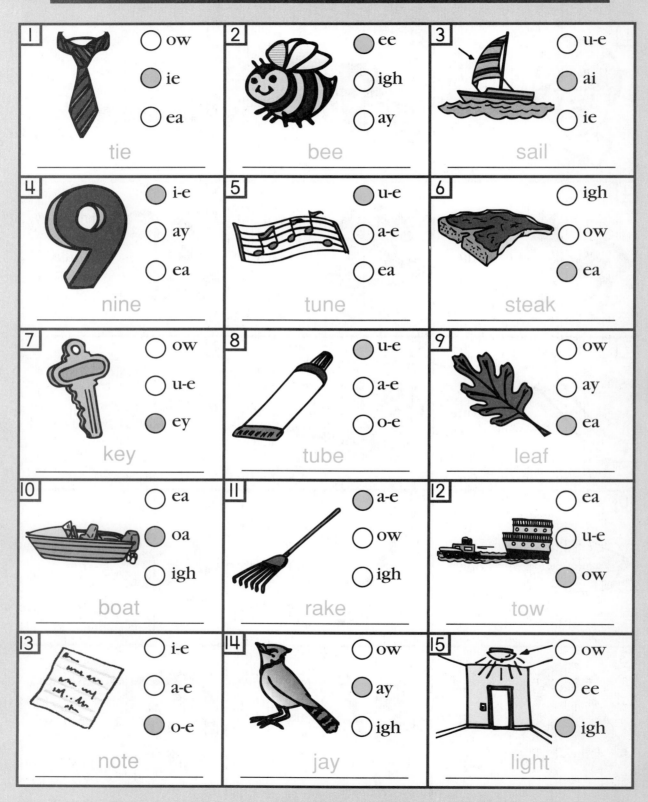

1. ○ ow ● ie ○ ea

tie

2. ● ee ○ igh ○ ay

bee

3. ○ u-e ● ai ○ ie

sail

4. ● i-e ○ ay ○ ea

nine

5. ● u-e ○ a-e ○ ea

tune

6. ○ igh ○ ow ● ea

steak

7. ○ ow ○ u-e ● ey

key

8. ● u-e ○ a-e ○ o-e

tube

9. ○ ow ○ ay ● ea

leaf

10. ○ ea ● oa ○ igh

boat

11. ● a-e ○ ow ○ igh

rake

12. ○ ea ○ u-e ● ow

tow

13. ○ i-e ○ a-e ● o-e

note

14. ○ ow ● ay ○ igh

jay

15. ○ ow ○ ee ● igh

light

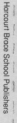

Read each word. If the word has a long vowel sound, circle *long*.
If the word has a short vowel sound, circle *short*.

REVIEW

1	hot	long / **short**

2	ring	long / **short**

3	game	**long** / short

4	belt	long / **short**

5	life	**long** / short

6	swim	long / **short**

7	sweet	**long** / short

8	camp	long / **short**

9	tent	long / **short**

10	flute	**long** / short

11	bowl	**long** / short

12	sight	**long** / short

13	trunk	long / **short**

14	sock	long / **short**

15	tune	**long** / short

16	pig	long / **short**

17	coal	**long** / short

18	young	long / **short**

19	treat	**long** / short

20	fry	**long** / short

REVIEW

Circle the name of each picture. Then write the word.

1. mart / mat / (mitt) _mitt_	2. (kite) / kit / kick _kite_	3. fan / fort / (feet) _feet_
4. (notes) / net / not _notes_	5. bead / (bed) / bad _bed_	6. it / eat / (eight) _eight_
7. tab / (tub) / tube _tub_	8. ran / rule / (rain) _rain_	9. (rod) / red / road _rod_
10. (man) / main / mean _man_	11. cat / (coat) / cot _coat_	12. sell / sale / (seal) _seal_
13. (mule) / mole / mail _mule_	14. cane / kind / (can) _can_	15. neat / (net) / night _net_

Review of Short and Long Vowels

Phonics Practice Book

Circle the word that best completes the sentence. Then write the word.

REVIEW

1. There are many ways to _____ride_____ between two places.

   rid   (ride)   road

2. You can go by rail on a _____train_____.

   (train)   tan   try

3. You can _____coast_____ down a slope on your bike.

   cost   cat   (coast)

4. You can row a boat down a _____stream_____.

   (stream)   stem   strap

5. You can _____fly_____ in a plane.

   fill   flea   (fly)

6. You _____might_____ like to take a bus.

   (might)   met   mitt

7. In the winter, ride in a _____sleigh_____ down a snowy path.

   slap   slid   (sleigh)

8. A jockey rides a _____fast_____ racing horse.

   face   (fast)   fist

9. Children might roller _____skate_____ down the sidewalk.

   scat   (skate)   skit

10. You might even ride a _____mule_____ on a dusty trail.

    (mule)   mug   mile

11. Of course, that would be a slow _____trip_____ .

    try   (trip)   tray

Fill in the circle next to the word that names each picture.

1		2		3	
	○ vain		○ tab		● tent
	● van		○ tub		○ tint
	○ phone		● tube		○ tone

4		5		6	
	○ club		● field		● ham
	○ call		○ fell		○ hum
	● colt		○ failed		○ home

7		8		9	
	○ shop		○ skate		○ rag
	● ship		○ skip		● rug
	○ shape		● sky		○ rage

10		11		12	
	● night		○ plow		○ big
	○ not		● play		○ bake
	○ neat		○ plead		● bag

13		14		15	
	● sock		● city		○ cube
	○ soak		○ sight		○ cob
	○ sick		○ kite		● cub

Harcourt Brace School Publishers

Fill in the circle next to the letter or letters that stand for the vowel sound in each picture name. Then write the word.

1
- ○ i
- ○ ai
- ○ i-e

six
_____

2
- ○ ay
- ○ igh
- ● ee

feet
_____

3
- ○ a
- ○ ie
- ○ u

cap
_____

4
- ○ ow
- ● a-e
- ○ o-e

cake
_____

5
- ○ u-e
- ○ i
- ● e

bed
_____

6
- ○ a-e
- ● i-e
- ○ ee

bike
_____

7
- ● o
- ○ ow
- ○ ay

mop
_____

8
- ○ e
- ○ i
- ● o-e

bone
_____

9
- ○ y
- ● u
- ○ ea

cup
_____

10
- ○ ai
- ○ y
- ● ow

snow
_____

11
- ○ oa
- ● ai
- ○ ey

rain
_____

12
- ● u
- ○ ee
- ○ u-e

sun
_____

13
- ○ ay
- ● ie
- ○ o

pie
_____

14
- ○ igh
- ○ o
- ● ea

leaf
_____

15
- ● u-e
- ○ a
- ○ ow

tube
_____

Name _____

Find the name of each picture. Write the word on the line.

shark	jar	harp	dart	artist	car	cart
barn	yarn	yard	arm	garden		

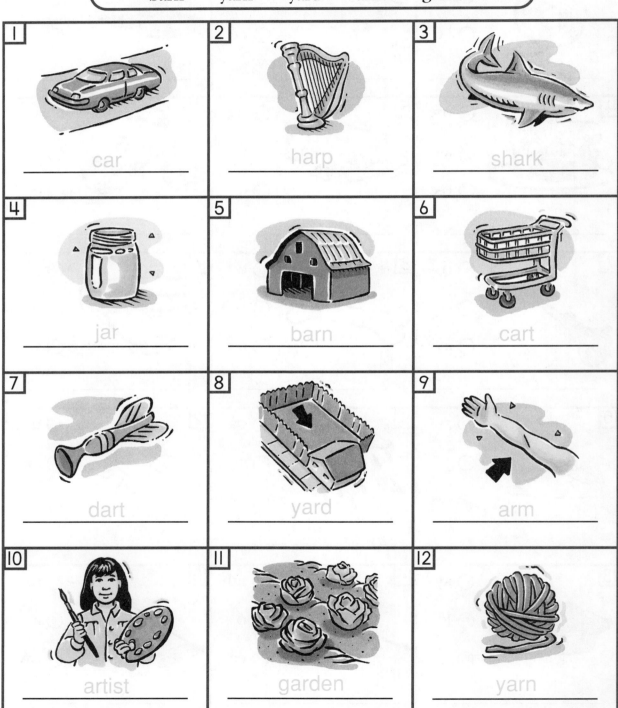

1. car

2. harp

3. shark

4. jar

5. barn

6. cart

7. dart

8. yard

9. arm

10. artist

11. garden

12. yarn

R-controlled Vowel: /är/*ar*

Phonics Practice Book

Harcourt Brace School Publishers

Choose the word that answers each riddle. Write the word on the line. You will not use all the words.

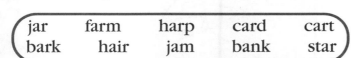

smart   shark   car   barn   score
park   chair   scarf   bean

1. I have sharp teeth and swim in the sea. I am a ____shark____.

2. I am a home for farm animals. I am a ____barn____.

3. When you get in, I can take you far. I am a ____car____.

4. You can play on my swings. I am bigger than your yard.

   I am a ____park____.

5. You wear me to keep warm. I am a ____scarf____.

jar   farm   harp   card   cart
bark   hair   jam   bank   star

6. Look for me in the sky when it's dark. I am a ____star____.

7. Many people say my music sounds pretty. I am a ____harp____.

8. My lid can be hard to open. I am a ____jar____.

9. I cover a tree trunk. I am ____bark____.

10. Shoppers put things in me. I am a ____cart____.

11. You get me in the mail on your birthday. I am a ____card____.

12. Work starts here when the animals wake up.

    I am a ____farm____.

Harcourt Brace School Publishers

Name _____

Find the name of each picture. Write the word on the line.

t<u>u</u>rkey

f<u>e</u>rn

hammer   tiger   spur   curl   letter   baker   turtle
purse   clerk   spur   shower   battery   baker   turkey

1	2	3
tiger	curl	hammer
4	**5**	**6**
turkey	letter	spur
7	**8**	**9**
baker	clerk	turtle
10	**11**	**12**
shower	purse	battery

Harcourt Brace School Publishers

R-controlled Vowel: /ûr/*er, ur*

Phonics Practice Book

Name _____

Write the word that completes the sentence.

curl   fur   turtle   sister   water

1. My _____sister_____ just got a new pet.

2. It's a big, brown _____turtle_____ .

3. She gives it plenty of _____water_____ .

4. My pet cat has soft, warm _____fur_____ .

5. I like to watch my cat _____curl_____ his tail.

person   turn   letter   her   term

6. I got a _____letter_____ in the mail.

7. It was from a _____person_____ I know.

8. She moved away last school _____term_____ .

9. I went to see _____her_____ new house.

10. Now it is her _____turn_____ to stay with me!

Name _____

bird

Write the word that names each picture.

| stir | dirt | thirty | girl | bird | shirt | third | skirt |

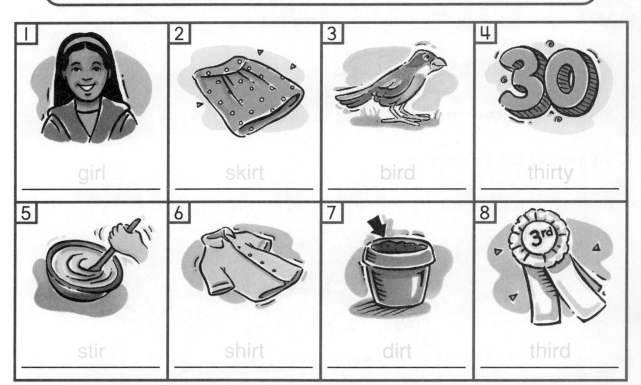

1. girl
2. skirt
3. bird
4. thirty
5. stir
6. shirt
7. dirt
8. third

Write the word that answers each clue. You will not use all the words.

| dirt | third | stir | dart | shirt | spur |

9. You might wear this with shorts. _____ shirt

10. If you are number three, you are this. _____ third

11. You might dig in this to make a garden. _____ dirt

12. You do this to mix a cake. _____ stir

R-controlled Vowel: /ûr/ *ir*

Phonics Practice Book

Look at the picture. Then do what the sentences tell you.

1. Add stripes to the woman's shirt.

2. Draw an X above the young girl.

3. Draw a box around the person who is third in line.

4. Show the sound the bird makes. Write *chirp* twice by the bird.

5. Circle the man's shirt.

6. Finish the girl's sentence. She calls the man *sir*.

7. Finish the price tag on the bird's cage. The bird costs thirty dollars.

Earth

Circle the sentence that best tells about each picture.

1.

We gave Mother a pearl necklace.

We gave Mother a pretty ring.

We earned the money to get a pet.

2.

The TV show came on early.

We heard the news on the radio.

We heard the news on TV.

3.

We heard a funny story.

We leave on buses after school.

We learn at school.

4.

I earn money by selling newspapers.

I like to ride my bike.

I learned how to play ball in gym class.

5.

I heard a thunderstorm.

I get up early every morning.

I eat breakfast every morning.

6.

We live in a house.

We earn money.

We are learning about planet Earth.

Harcourt Brace School Publishers

Read the story. Then answer the questions.

Jack's Fishing Trip

One day Jack went to visit his aunt and uncle. His uncle Earl and his aunt Pearl were very happy to see him.

Jack said he wanted to learn to fish. Earl promised to take him early the next morning. So Pearl packed some lunch for Jack and Earl and wished them good luck.

Jack was very excited as he heard the motor on the boat start with a loud *varoom.* That morning Jack caught three fish. Earl said Jack learned very quickly.

When they got home that night, Earl and Jack cleaned the fish. Jack helped Pearl cook them. Earl gave Jack his very own fishing pole. Earl told Jack that he had earned it! Jack cannot wait until his next visit!

Possible responses are shown.

1. Why do you think Aunt Pearl and Uncle Earl were glad to see Jack?

   They love him.

   _____

2. For how long did Jack and his uncle fish?

   all day

   _____

3. What did Jack learn to do very quickly?

   He learned to catch fish.

   _____

4. How did Jack earn his own fishing pole?

   He caught fish, cleaned them, and helped cook them.

   _____

Harcourt Brace School Publishers

Name _____

Choose the word that fits each clue. Write the word in the puzzle.

car   jar   fur   bird   earth   shark
skirt   fern   curl   pearl

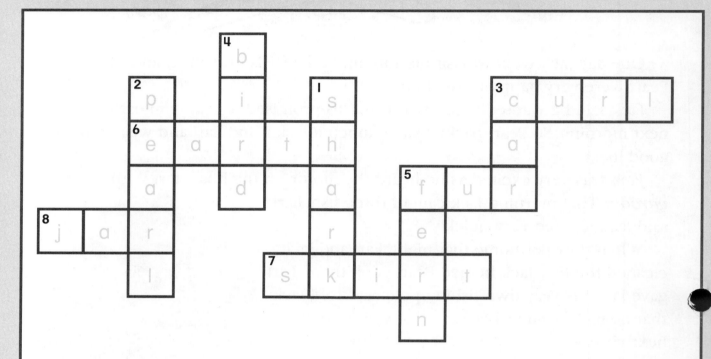

Across

3. What some people's hair can do

5. Something soft and warm

6. The planet we live on

7. Something you wear

8. You can keep many different things in this

Down

1. A fish with sharp teeth

2. A shiny, round stone

3. Something you ride in

4. An animal that lives in a tree

5. A plant with thin, green leaves

Review of *R*-controlled Vowels: /är/*ar*; /ûr/*er, ur, ir, ear*

Phonics Practice Book

Harcourt Brace School Publishers

Name _____

REVIEW

shirt	skirt	farmer	yard	artist	earth	scarf	shark
park	tiger	bird	barn	turtle	writer	teacher	sweater

1 Which are animals?

shark

tiger

bird

turtle

2 Which are places?

yard

earth

park

barn

3 Which are things you can wear?

shirt

skirt

scarf

sweater

4 Which are people?

farmer

artist

writer

teacher

Choose the word that answers each riddle. Write the word.

5. I swim in the ocean and have sharp teeth. I am a _____ shark _____ .

6. I have many trees, flowers, and benches in me. I am a _____ park _____ .

7. You wear me. Sometimes I have long sleeves. I am a _____ shirt _____ .

8. I have cows and horses in my barn. I am a _____ farmer _____ .

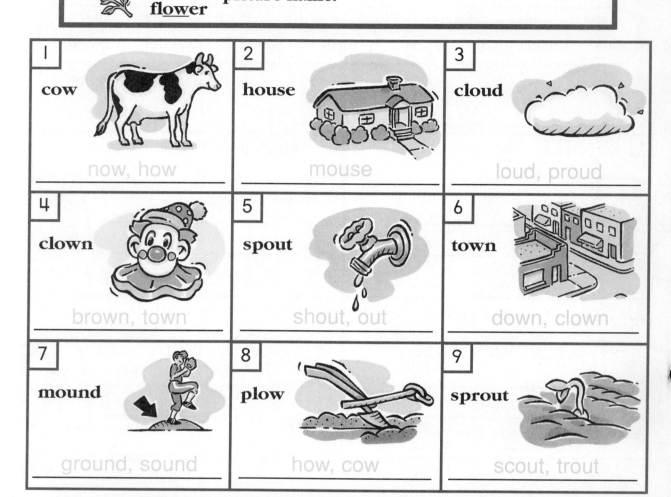

cloud

flower

Possible responses are shown.

Write a word that rhymes with each picture name.

1 cow — now, how	**2** house — mouse	**3** cloud — loud, proud
4 clown — brown, town	**5** spout — shout, out	**6** town — down, clown
7 mound — ground, sound	**8** plow — how, cow	**9** sprout — scout, trout

Look at the pictures again. Do what the sentences tell you.

10. Draw a bell around the neck of the cow.
    bell drawn around the cow's neck

11. Draw a flower next to the house.
    flower drawn next to the house

12. Give the clown a mouth.
    mouth drawn on clown

Vowel Diphthong: /ou/ *ow, ou*   Phonics Practice Book

Harcourt Brace School Publishers

Name _____

| blouse | towel | couch | plow | crowd | hound |

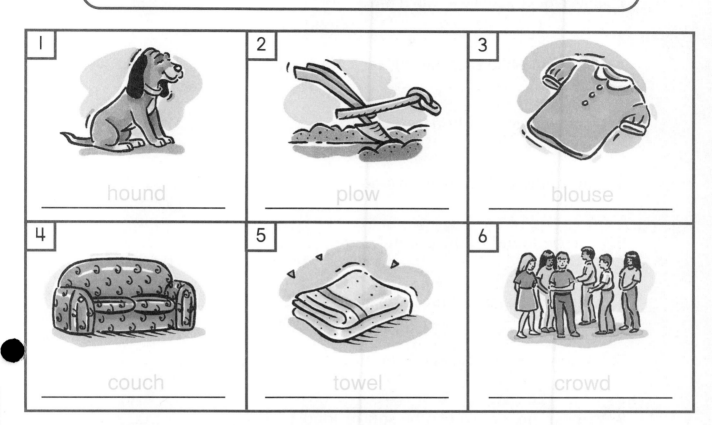

1. hound

2. plow

3. blouse

4. couch

5. towel

6. crowd

Choose the word that fits each sentence. Write the word.

| bow | down | mouse | blouse | south | hour |

7. My pet __mouse__ likes to eat cheese.

8. Juan thanked the crowd and then took a __bow__.

9. Janie wore a brown skirt and a pretty white __blouse__.

10. Artie put his book __down__ and went to sleep.

11. Kim can play outdoors for one __hour__.

12. Eric lives __south__ of the lake.

Name _____

1. Rain falls down from me. I am a _____cloud_____.

   cloud   clown   club

2. You would like the milk I give! I am a _____cow_____.

   couch   cow   cub

3. I have streets and houses. I am a _____town_____.

   ton   towel   town

4. I am funny when I play around. I am a _____clown_____.

   clue   cloud   clown

5. I can be found in the ground. I am a _____flower_____.

   flower   follow   float

6. Water comes out of me. I am a _____spout_____.

   shout   spout   sport

7. I hide when the cat is on the prowl. I am a _____mouse_____.

   most   mound   mouse

8. You can hear me. I can be soft or loud. I am a _____sound_____.

   south   sound   snow

9. When you sit down, you might use me. I am a _____couch_____.

   couch   cloud   cube

10. I am proud to rest on the king's head. I am a _____crown_____.

    church   crown   crew

11. I can fly down from a tree. I am an _____owl_____..

    oil   owl   vowel

12. I am a good pet to have around when something needs to be

    found. I am a _____hound_____.

    hut   house   hound

Vowel Diphthong: /ou/ow, ou

Harcourt Brace School Publishers

Phonics Practice Book

Name_____

Lost and Found

For four days the clouds were dark and the rain came down. Mom and I stayed in the house. We watched the raindrops bounce off the ground. We listened to the sounds of the storm.

The next day was sunny. We were invited to go camping with the Brown family. When we got to the camp, my dog Scout jumped out of the car. He ran down the mountain and into some trees.

"How will we ever find him?" I cried. We looked around the area for Scout, but did not see him. He was not to be found!

Then we heard a loud sound in a bush—a dog's howl! It was Scout! I was so glad that we had found him. Well, maybe Scout really found us. He looked so proud.

Write the answers to the questions.

Possible responses are shown.

1. What problem did the boy and his mom have at the camp?

   They couldn't find their dog, Scout.

2. What happened to Scout?

   He jumped out of the car and ran down the mountain.

3. Why did Scout look proud?

   He found the boy and his mom.

Name _____

cord   shore   four

Circle the letters that complete the picture name. Write the letters on the line.

1	ore (ire) are	st _ore_

2 or ea er   st _or_ k

3 ou or ir   c _or_ d

4 or ur ou   st _or_ m

5 or ea ar   p _or_ ch

6 or ou ar   m _or_ ning

7 ire (our) are   f _our_

8 (ore) eer are   c _ore_

9 ear (our) are   p _our_

10 ir ee (or)   t _or_ n

11 oo (or) er   th _or_ n

12 or er ar   h _or_ n

13 (ore) ur are   sn _ore_

14 ar er (or)   c _or_ n

15 (or) ou ar   h _or_ se

R-controlled Vowel: /ôr/*or, ore, our*   Phonics Practice Book

Name _____

 door

 soar

**Circle the word that completes the sentence.
Then write the word.**

1. Our family was going to the lake. We locked the front

   _____door_____ and left.

   (door) down   done   dirt

2. We were going to use our rowboat. My brother and I each carried

   an _____oar_____ .

   oat (oar) oak   oath

3. Near the boat, we saw a hurt bird. Mom said,

   "_____Poor_____ thing."

   pair   roof   rope (poor)

4. We found a box and put the bird in it. "We will help you," we said.

   "Soon you will _____soar_____ high in the sky."

   sort (soar) some   soon

5. Soon the bird was better. We saw it hop around on the

   _____floor_____ .

   flame (floor) flop   flour

6. We made a ramp for the bird with a _____board_____ .

   (board) bread   bore   boat

7. As we watched the bird fly away, we heard a loud sound. "Was that

   a _____roar_____ ?" Mom asked.

   roam   road (roar) rear

8. "No, it's just our dog," said my brother. "He's just

   thumping his tail on the _____floor_____ ."

   food (floor) fish   for

R-controlled Vowel /ôr/*oor, oar*   143

Name _____

Write the word that names each picture.

clown   house   cord   oar   corn
spout   door   stork   four

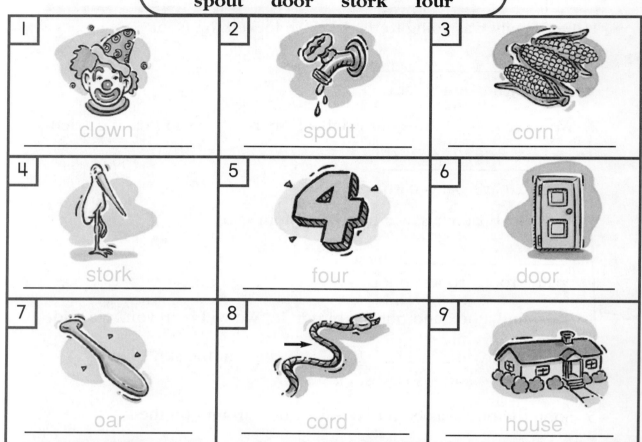

1. clown
2. spout
3. corn
4. stork
5. four
6. door
7. oar
8. cord
9. house

Answer the riddles with words that rhyme. You will not use all of the words.

oar   pour   house   cow

10. What do you say to a farm animal when you want something fast?

"Now, _____ cow _____!"

11. What do you call the home of a tiny animal that loves cheese?

a mouse _____ house _____

12. What do you call a shop that sells paddles?

an _____ oar _____ store

Review of Diphthong /ou/ow, ou,
R-controlled Vowel: /ôr/or, ore, our, oor, oar

Phonics Practice Book

Name _____

Choose the word that completes each sentence. Then write the word in the puzzle.

| door | four | store | found | cow | town |
| roar | stork | mouse | loud | shore | torn | soar |

ACROSS

2. If you have two pairs of socks, you have _____ socks.

3. We live in a small _____ , not a city.

5. This paper is _____ in half.

6. Will you please open the _____ for me?

9. When we go to the beach, we will play on the _____ .

11. Gail got a new toy at the _____ .

DOWN

1. Did you feed the big brown _____ ?

2. Peter _____ a penny and picked it up.

4. The story is about a tiny white _____ who rides a bike.

7. The lion gave a big _____ .

8. Our teacher says, "Be quiet! You are too _____ ."

9. We saw a plane _____ through the sky.

10. A _____ is a tall bird.

Phonics Practice Book
Review of Diphthong: /ou/ow, ou;
R-Controlled Vowel: /ôr/or, ore, our, oor, oar
145

coin

toy

Put a ✔ under each picture whose name has the vowel sound you hear in *coin* and *toy*.

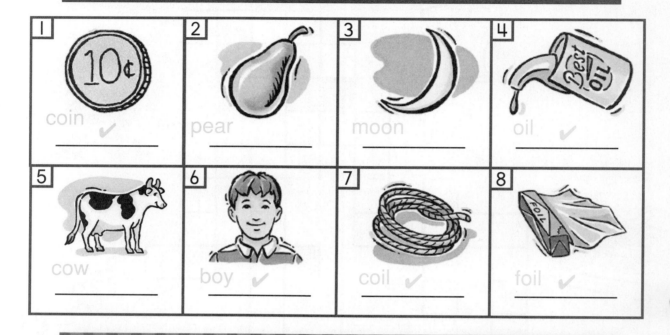

| 1 coin ✔ | 2 pear | 3 moon | 4 oil ✔ |
| 5 cow | 6 boy ✔ | 7 coil ✔ | 8 foil ✔ |

Circle the word that names the picture. Then write the word on the line.

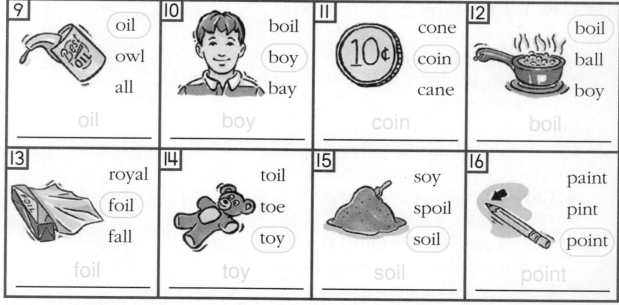

| 9 oil / owl / all — oil | 10 boil / boy / bay — boy | 11 cone / coin / cane — coin | 12 boil / ball / boy — boil |
| 13 royal / foil / fall — foil | 14 toil / toe / toy — toy | 15 soy / spoil / soil — soil | 16 paint / pint / point — point |

Vowel Diphthong: /oi/*oi, oy*

Phonics Practice Book

Write the word that names each picture. You will not use all of the words.

foil   boil   cowboy   coil   toy   soy
soil   point   oil   coin   boy

1. soil
2. boil
3. foil
4. toy
5. coin
6. boy
7. oil
8. point

Now use some of the words from above to complete these sentences.

9. I like to play with the _____boy_____ next door.

10. Mom let me buy a new _____toy_____ to share with him.

11. I chose a little car. It is fast, but it does not need gas or

_____oil_____.

12. I hope my friend will like the car. I used my last _____coin_____

to pay for it.

Name _____

Write a word with *oi* or *oy* to answer each question.

1. What is at the end of a sharp pencil and rhymes with *joint*?
   _____point_____

2. What word names a person who is not a girl? It rhymes with *toy*.
   _____boy_____

3. What is another way to cook things that rhymes with *broil*?
   _____boil_____

4. What word means "to put things together" and rhymes with *coin*?
   _____join_____

5. What do you call a king and queen and their family? It rhymes with
   loyal. _____royal_____

6. What kind of silver paper shines and rhymes with *coil*?
   _____foil_____

7. What is a thing to play with that rhymes with *joy*? _____toy_____

8. What word names the shape of a rope or a curled-up snake and rhymes
   with *toil*? _____coil_____

9. What word means "a little wet" and rhymes with *hoist*?
   _____moist_____

10. What word means "happiness" and rhymes with *toy*?
    _____joy_____

11. What names something that you can spend or save and rhymes with
    join? _____coin_____

12. What do plants grow in? Its name rhymes with *coil*. _____soil_____

Vowel Diphthong: /oi/*oi*, *oy*

Phonics Practice Book

Harcourt Brace School Publishers

Name _____

Dad said I could invite a friend to join us for dinner, so I asked my pal Roy. He is the best friend a boy could have. He is smart, funny, and loyal.

When Roy got here, we were hungry. We helped Dad cook dinner. Dad broiled sirloin steak. He put some foil on a pan and sprinkled soy sauce on the steak. He put the sirloin under the broiler. Roy and I snapped fresh beans and put them in a pot to boil. After a while, the steak was done. Dad said it looked nice and moist.

When we sat down to eat, Dad said our meal looked like a royal feast. Did we ever enjoy it! The food was good, and everyone laughed and talked. After we helped Dad clean up, we went to play with my toys. When Roy left, he said he had enjoyed himself. He asked me to join his family for dinner one day soon. Oh, boy!

Possible responses are shown.

1. What would be a good title for the story? Titles should reflect the main idea of the story. Possible titles might be Good Friend, Good Food or My Favorite Meal.

2. Why did everyone enjoy the meal? The food was good, and everyone laughed and talked.

3. Why is Roy a good friend? He is smart, funny, and loyal.

4. What did the boys do to help Dad cook? They snapped beans and put them in a pot to boil. They helped Dad clean up.

I would like this book.

CHECK OUT

The letters *ou* in *would* and the letters *oo* in *book* stand for the same vowel sound. Write the word that names each picture.

book   brook   hook   wood

1.  book

2.  wood

3.  hook

4.  brook

Write *yes* or *no* to answer each question. Then circle each word that has the vowel sound you hear in *cook* and *could*.

5. Should you take a good look before crossing the street? _____ yes

6. Could a book swim in a brook? _____ no

7. Would a fishhook fit in a hood? _____ yes

8. Could a coat made of wool keep you warm? _____ yes

9. If you took a log and made a chair, would the chair be made of wood? _____ yes

10. Could someone cook a fish on a wood fire? _____ yes

11. Should you wear a wool hood to keep cool? _____ no

Harcourt Brace School Publishers

The words below are in the puzzle. Some words go down, and some go across. Find and circle each one.

took	should	look	cookie	foot	would
could	brook	hook	stood	shook	hood
	cook	book	wool	wood	

a	b	c	o	o	k	i	e	d	e	w	f	h
s	h	o	u	l	d	d	g	b	r	o	o	k
h	o	u	s	s	v	s	c	o	h	o	l	r
o	o	l	o	o	k	o	c	o	u	l	d	w
o	d	d	b	s	t	o	o	k	l	s	r	o
k	s	v	f	o	o	t	o	h	o	o	k	o
w	o	u	l	d	b	x	k	s	t	o	o	d

Write the word from the puzzle that names each picture. You will not use all of the words.

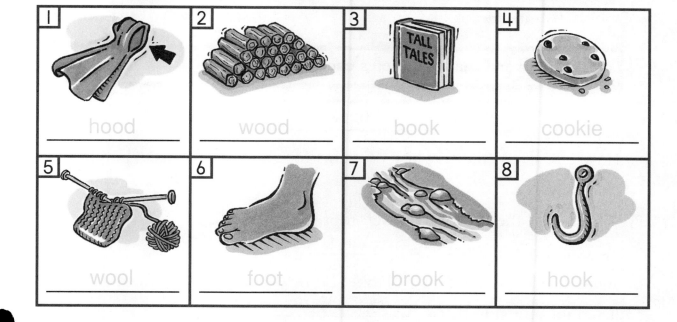

1. hood
2. wood
3. book
4. cookie
5. wool
6. foot
7. brook
8. hook

Name _____

REVIEW

Do what the sentences tell you.

1. Circle the cowboy's hat.   cowboy's hat is circled

2. Add a piece of wood to the fire.   wood drawn on fire

3. Draw a small bush in the soil.   bush drawn in soil

4. Mark an X on the coil of rope.   X marked on rope

5. Draw a fish in the brook.   fish drawn in brook

Write the word that completes each sentence.

(soil   wool   book   broil   look)

6. How else could the cowboy cook his food?

He could _____broil_____ it.

7. What could the cowboy do before it gets dark?

He could read his _____book_____ .

8. What would the cowboy's blanket be made of if it came from a sheep?

It would be made of _____wool_____ .

Review of Vowel Diphthong: /oi/oi, oy;
Vowel Variant: /oo̅/oo, ou • Reading Words in Context

Phonics Practice Book

Harcourt Brace School Publishers

Name _____

Write the word that names each picture. You will not use all of the words.

boy   boil   toy   soil   oil   wool   royal   point
book   foil   coil   brook   hood   wood   hook

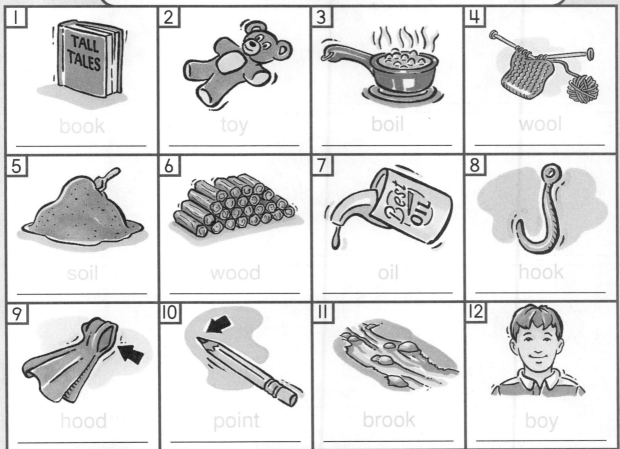

1	2	3	4
book	toy	boil	wool

5	6	7	8
soil	wood	oil	hook

9	10	11	12
hood	point	brook	boy

Use some of the words you wrote to complete these sentences.

13. Troy does not want to
    play with his ____toy____ .

14. He wishes he could
    fish in the ____brook____ .

15. He should have brought his
    pole and ____hook____ .

16. Then he would have been a happy ____boy____ .

Circle the letters that complete each picture name. Then write the letters.

1 er / ir / (ar)

c ar _____

2 (er) / oi / ar

tig er _____

3 or / ou / (ur)

sp ur _____

4 ar / oo / (ir)

sh ir t _____

5 (ear) / ir / ar

ear th _____

6 oo / (ow) / or

cl ow n _____

7 oy / or / (ou)

h ou se _____

8 ar / oi / (or)

w or m _____

9 ar / ear / (ore)

st ore _____

10 (our) / ear / ow

f our _____

11 ow / (oor) / ear

d oor _____

12 ear / ou / (oar)

s oar _____

13 ir / (oi) / oo

c oi n _____

14 ou / oo / (oy)

b oy _____

15 oi / (oo) / ow

b oo k _____

Cumulative Review of *R*-controlled Vowels: /är/*ar*; /ûr/*er, ur, ir, ear*; /ôr/*or, ore, our, oor, oar*; Vowel Diphthong: /ou/*ow, ou;* /oi/*oi, oy*; Vowel Variant: /o͞o/*oo, ou*

Phonics Practice Book

Circle the name of each picture. Then write the word.

1.

card
curt
(card)
card

2.

shovel
shopper
(shower)
shower

3.

pore
(purse)
power
purse

4.

scarf
skit
(skirt)
skirt

5.

earn
(earth)
each
earth

6.

call
(cow)
car
cow

7.

(house)
hose
haze
house

8.

ham
(horn)
howl
horn

9.

star
stir
(store)
store

10.
four
far
fir
four

11.

deep
day
(door)
door

12.

oak
(oar)
oats
oar

13.
oil
oar
order
oil

14.
box
(boy)
bay
boy

15.
bark
beak
(book)
book

Cumulative Review of *R*-controlled Vowels: /är/*ar*; /ûr/*er, ur, ir, ear*; /ôr/*or, ore, our, oor, oar*; Vowel Diphthong: /ou/*ow, ou*; /oi/*oi, oy*; Vowel Variant: /o͞o/*oo, ou*

beard

deer

Circle the word that completes the sentence. Write the word on the line.

1. Today was to be the biggest day of the _____year_____.

   your   yard   (year)

2. Our team had a game. We had all our _____gear_____ ready.

   (gear)   germ   grow

3. When I got up, I could _____hear_____ a noise.

   (hear)   hair   hurt

4. I went to _____peer_____ outside to see what it was.

   (peer)   park   pour

5. I had a _____fear_____ that it was rain, and I was right.

   fair   (fear)   fir

6. I called a friend who lives _____near_____ me.

   now   (near)   need

7. While we were talking, she let out a _____cheer_____.

   cheat   (cheer)   chair

8. She had looked outside and seen a young _____deer_____.

   (deer)   dart   dent

9. "What a _____dear_____ little animal!" she said, as he ran off.

   dare   dial   (dear)

10. Soon the rain stopped, and the sky grew _____clear_____.

    We could play our game!   (clear)   clerk   claim

Name _____

Circle the name of each picture. Then write the word.

1	
shares (stairs) starts	

stairs
_____

2	
spare part (pear)	

pear
_____

3	
(mare) mint main	

mare
_____

4	
hang hire (hare)	

hare
_____

5	
heat hate (hair)	

hair
_____

6	
(bear) beast beard	

bear
_____

7	
tart (tear) target	

tear
_____

8	
barn (bare) bake	

bare
_____

9	
(share) shack shirt	

share
_____

10	
chart (chair) chain	

chair
_____

11	
(square) spray squire	

square
_____

12	
earn (air) aim	

air
_____

Name _____

We have pear trees on our farm. In the winter the trees are bare. In the spring they have flowers that make the air smell nice. In the summer the trees are full of pears. When the trees have pears, my friend and I help pick them.

We get up on chairs to reach the pears. We pick all we can reach. I save a few for Clair, my mare. My friend gives some to his pet hare, Carey. We walk back to the house and sit on the stairs to eat our good, sweet pears.

Write the answers to the questions.

1. What would be a good title for the story?

   Responses will vary.

2. How do the trees change during the year?

   In the winter they are bare; in the spring they have flowers;

   in the summer they have pears.

3. Who eats the pears?

   the children, the mare, the pet hare

R-controlled Vowel: /âr/*air, ear, are* • Reading Words in Context   Phonics Practice Book

Harcourt Brace School Publishers

Read the sentences and do what they tell you.

1. Write the year under the words *State Fair*.

   a year written under the words State Fair

2. Circle what the girl will wear.

   prize ribbon circled

3. Draw a line under those who give a cheer.

   people cheering underlined

4. Put an X on the mare.

   the mare marked with an X

5. Draw a pair of eyeglasses on the girl.

   a pair of glasses drawn on the girl

6. Put a big dot near the steer.

   a dot drawn near the steer

7. Mark a check (✔) over the man with a beard.

   man with beard marked with a [✔]

8. Put a box around the boy near the steer.

   box drawn around child nearest the steer

9. Write *deer* on the deer's pen.

   deer written on deer's pen

10. Draw leaves on the bare tree.

    leaves drawn on the tree

Review of *R*-controlled Vowels: /ir/*ear, eer*; /âr/*air, ear, are*

Harcourt Brace School Publishers

Name _____

Read the poem, and answer the questions.

The Camping Trip

The air is crisp.
The sky is fair.
We drive from the city
Without a care.

We unpack our gear,
Our tent big and square.
I've broken a chair,
But Mom packed a spare.

We dare the dark woods,
Just hoping to see
A soft, little hare
Or a deer wild and free.

We break up our camp,
For school days are near.
We are sad to go home,
But we'll come back next year!

1. What is the weather like for the trip?
   The air is crisp and the sky is fair.

2. What do the campers hope to see in the woods?
   a hare or a deer

3. Why are there still enough chairs?
   Mom packed a spare.

Review of R-controlled Vowels: /ir/ *ear, eer*; /âr/ *air, ear, are*   Phonics Practice Book

Name _____

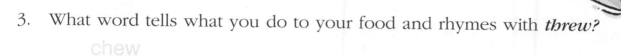

flew

blue

Write an *ew* or a *ue* word to answer each question.

1. What is a color that rhymes with *glue?* _____blue_____

2. What can help you solve a mystery? It rhymes with *true*.
   _____clue_____

3. What word tells what you do to your food and rhymes with *threw?*
   _____chew_____

4. What can you eat with a spoon that rhymes with *few?*
   _____stew_____

5. What do you call a team of people who work together?
   It rhymes with *grew*. _____crew_____

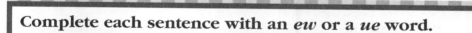

Complete each sentence with an *ew* or a *ue* word.

6. My sister lost her ring. She did not have a _____clue_____ where
   to find it.

7. She said, "I had it when I was helping Dad make _____stew_____
   for supper."

8. "Maybe you threw it out with the peels in the _____blue_____
   trash bag," I said.

9. "That must be it!" she said. We ran home to check the bag before the
   garbage _____crew_____ picked it up.

Harcourt Brace School Publishers

Name _____

Circle the word that answers each riddle. Write the word on the line.

1. I am the color of the sky on a bright, clear day. I am _____blue_____.

   bloom (blue) blank

2. When you do not know something, I help you find it out. I am a _____clue_____.

   chew (clue) coop

3. I am a boy, and I have an aunt. I am her _____nephew_____.

   (nephew) noon next

4. I make things stick to paper. I am _____glue_____.

   glare gleam (glue)

5. You can walk down me because I am like a street. I am an _____avenue_____.

   afternoon (avenue) animal

6. I am a special kind of stone you can wear. I am a _____jewel_____.

   (jewel) jeep juice

7. I am a thick soup with carrots, potatoes, and meat. I am a _____stew_____.

   (stew) stool street

8. When you read me, I tell you about things that have happened. I am the _____news_____.

   near (news) noise

Vowel Variant: /oo/ue, ew

Phonics Practice Book

Harcourt Brace School Publishers

Read the book titles. Look for words that have the vowel sound you hear in the words _grew_ and _glue_. Then write the words under the correct heading.

Words with _ew_, like _grew_

stew

blew

jewel

Words that end with _ue_, like _glue_

true

clue

blue

Possible responses are shown.

Write the answers to the questions.

1. Which book probably has many stories in it?

Story Stew

2. Which book is a mystery?

The Clue in the Basement

3. Which book is not a fantasy?

A True Story

Name _____

When I Flew to Aunt Sue's

My grandmother took me to visit my aunt in Arizona. Grandmother says I am Aunt Sue's favorite nephew. I know it is true because I am Aunt Sue's only nephew. I knew we would have fun.

It was my first plane trip. We flew in a big jet. As the plane went up, I looked out the window. The cars and houses below grew smaller. Then we were high in the sky. It looked very blue.

When the plane landed, the crew came out to greet us. They said to come back soon. Grandmother said we would, since we were due home next week.

Possible responses are shown.

Write the answers to the questions.

1. How does the boy know he is Aunt Sue's favorite nephew?

   He is her only nephew.

2. What were the two reasons that the boy wanted to go to Aunt Sue's?

   He knew they would have fun; it was his first plane trip.

moon

Write the word from the box that names
the picture.

igloo	goose	boot	broom
stool	spoon	roof	kangaroo

1	2	3	4
broom	spoon	roof	goose

5	6	7	8
kangaroo	igloo	boot	stool

Circle the words that have the same vowel sound as *moon*.
Then write the words.

book	(tooth)	brook	(pool)	(food)
(zoo)	hood	(school)	wool	wood

zoo   pool

tooth   food

school

Harcourt Brace School Publishers

Name _____

Scouts in the Afternoon

All day at school, I was in a good mood. I knew that in the afternoon I would meet with my scout troop at the park. Our leader, Ms. Moon, would read to us from our scout book. Then we would pick up trash and take turns sweeping the sidewalk with a broom. Later we might shoot some hoops. Ms. Moon might even take us for a swim in the pool. One time she took us to the zoo.

Then we would have a snack. I brought the food. My mom and I made cookies. I knew those cookies were good. Everyone in my troop has a sweet tooth! The afternoon could not come too soon!

Possible responses are shown.

Write the answers to the questions.

1. Why was the girl in a good mood all day?

   She knew she would meet with her scout troop in the afternoon.

2. What are two things the scouts do at the park to help others?

   They pick up trash and sweep the sidewalk.

Harcourt Brace School Publishers

soup

fr<u>ui</u>t

Circle the word that fits the clue.

1. It is a black-and-blue mark on your skin.

   brook   (bruise)   buses

2. You use a spoon to eat this.

   (soup)   soon   sew

3. It is a trip you take on a ship.

   crew   cool   (cruise)

4. It is a large member of the cat family.

   coop   (cougar)   could

5. Lemons, apples, and pears are this.

   fright   frisky   (fruit)

6. This can be a matching jacket and pants.

   (suit)   soup   sure

7. You might drink this in the morning.

   jewel   junk   (juice)

8. This tells about more than one.

   grew   gloom   (group)

Look at the words you circled. Can you find three pairs of rhyming words? Write them on the lines below.

-oup	-uit	-uise
soup	suit	cruise
group	fruit	bruise

Circle the sentence that tells about the picture.

1. Drew stirs the soup with a big spoon.

   Drew steers the spaceship to the moon.

   Drew shoots the ball through the hoop.

2. Drew says the moon will be out soon.

   Drew says the soup will be done at noon.

   Drew says he needs a new tool.

3. Sue will fix the screw.

   Sue will join the crew.

   Sue will sit on a stool.

4. They have to look for their jewels.

   They have to let their soup cool.

   They have to see how much they grew.

5. Drew will help Sue blow up the balloon.

   Drew will help Sue clean up the room.

   Drew will help Sue look for the clue.

6. Drew sweeps with the broom.

   Drew has a good time at the zoo.

   Drew has a big, blue bruise.

Use words from the box to answer the questions.

kangaroo   fruit   school   suit   juice
moose   stew   boot   zoo   cougar
soup   pool   goose   jewel

1 **Which are animals?**

kangaroo
_____
moose
_____
cougar
_____
goose
_____

2 **Which are things to eat or drink?**

fruit
_____
juice
_____
stew
_____
soup
_____

3 **Which are places?**

school
_____
zoo
_____
pool
_____

4 **Which are things to wear?**

suit
_____
boot
_____
jewel
_____

1,000 thousand   **table**   **hammer**   Circle the word that names each picture. Then write the word.

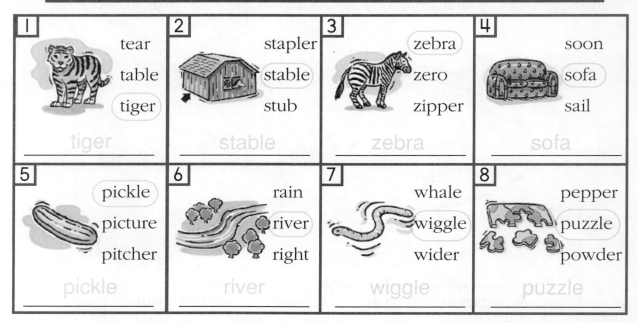

1.
tear
table
(tiger)

tiger

2.
stapler
(stable)
stub

stable

3.
(zebra)
zero
zipper

zebra

4.
soon
(sofa)
sail

sofa

5.
(pickle)
picture
pitcher

pickle

6.
rain
(river)
right

river

7.
whale
(wiggle)
wider

wiggle

8.
pepper
(puzzle)
powder

puzzle

Use some of the words you wrote to answer the clues.

9. You sit on this. _____ sofa _____

10. People put one of these together for fun. _____ puzzle _____

11. You should stay away from this animal if it is hungry. _____ tiger _____

12. This food may be sweet or salty, but it is always crunchy.
_____ pickle _____

13. The black-and-white stripes of this animal make it look special.
_____ zebra _____

14. This body of water sometimes leads to the sea. _____ river _____

15. This is a place where horses are kept. _____ stable _____

Name _____

Read the selection to learn about animals in danger.

Animals in Danger

Many kinds of animals in the world are in danger of dying out. Long ago, large herds of zebra could be seen in Africa. Now there are fewer of them because some hunters do not obey the law. Another animal in danger is the tiger. Many tigers lose their homes when people clear the jungle where the tigers live.

What other animal home is in danger? Ask the sea turtle. It is sometimes caught in fishers' nets. Litter in the sea has also harmed the turtle. These animals are in terrible danger. Some of these animals can be saved if people work to help protect them.

Write the answers to the questions.

Possible responses are shown.

1. What is the selection about?

   animals in danger

2. Why is the zebra in danger?

   Some hunters do not obey the law.

3. What are two dangers for the sea turtle?

   fishers' nets and litter

4. How does the story say the animals can be saved?

   People can work to help protect them.

Write the word that names each picture.

fawn **taught** **bought**

caught   lawn   yawn   crawl   paw   hawk

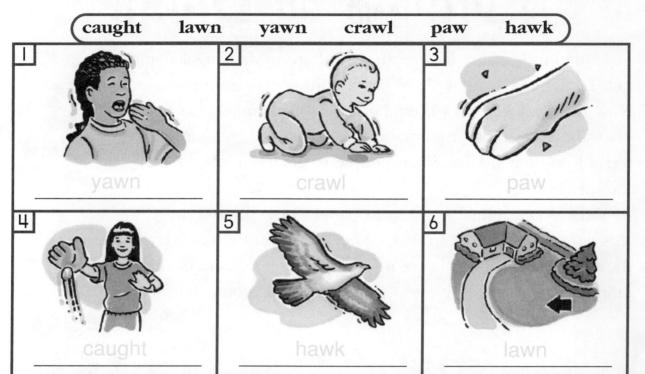

1. yawn
2. crawl
3. paw
4. caught
5. hawk
6. lawn

Circle the word that the sentence tells about.

7. If you grabbed a ball from the air, you could say you did this.

   (caught)   call   could

8. If you are tired, you might do this with your mouth.

   yard   (yawn)   yellow

9. If someone helped you learn something, he or she did this.

   tweak   tooth   (taught)

10. If someone feels that you should do something, he or she might use this word in telling you about it.

    oat   (ought)   odd

Name _____

Write *yes* or *no* to answer each question.

1. Does a goldfish have a claw? _____no_____

2. Can a hawk play the piano? _____no_____

3. Should you yawn during dinner? _____no_____

4. Do bunnies have soft paws? _____yes_____

5. Can a fawn fly in the sky? _____no_____

6. Should you let a rhino on your lawn? _____no_____

Choose the word that completes each sentence. Write the word.

7. My sister Dawn and I went to the river to go fishing. We saw a

_____fawn_____ with a fluffy, white tail.

⟨fawn⟩   found   fan

8. We usually do not agree on the kind of fishing bait to use, but we have

never _____fought_____ about it.

fruit   ⟨fought⟩   foot

9. Dawn must have chosen the right bait, because she _____caught_____

the fish.

cow   crow   ⟨caught⟩

10. We did not stay a long time. We had gotten up early, and I started to

_____yawn_____.

⟨yawn⟩   yard   yarn

Vowel Variant: /ô/ *aw, au(gh), ou(gh)*   **173**

Read the story, and think about what happens.

The Surprise in the Woods

Grandpa and I got up at dawn and went into the woods. We wanted to see some animals. We thought we might see some birds and a few squirrels. Were we ever surprised by what we saw!

When we sat down for a rest, I saw something moving in the trees. I was not sure what it was. Then I knew. It was a bear! It had long, sharp claws, and big, strong jaws. I told Grandpa we ought to go. Just then, the bear ran away. Was I ever glad! That bear taught me that I ought to be careful when I'm in the woods.

Write the answers to the questions.

Possible responses are shown.

1. Why did the boy and his grandpa go into the woods?

   They wanted to see some animals.

2. What surprising thing did they see?

   a bear

3. What happened that made the boy glad?

   The bear ran away.

Vowel Variant: /ô/*aw, augh, ough* • Reading Words in Context   Phonics Practice Book

Harcourt Brace School Publishers

Name _____

He ____ it!

1. Circle the person who is learning to crawl.
   baby is circled

2. The baby has just caught a ball. Draw the ball in his hands.
   ball is drawn in the baby's hands

3. Draw a line under the person who has taught the baby to catch.
   line is drawn under the mother

4. Finish the mother's thought.
   caught is written in the thought bubble

5. Put an X on the new thing the mother bought for the baby.
   an X is drawn on the new suit

6. Circle the thing the mother ought to give the baby when he is hungry.
   bottle is circled

7. Draw a pillow in the place where the mother will put the baby when

   he begins to yawn. pillow is drawn in the crib

8. Circle the puppy's paws. dog's paws are circled

9. Draw a window in the room that shows the front lawn.
   window showing the lawn is drawn

Name _____

Write the word that names each picture.

bought	crawl	caught	hammer	taught
zipper	salad	fawn	table	thousand
sofa	thought	straw	puzzle	butter

1 puzzle	**2** taught	**3** fawn
4 zipper	**5** sofa	**6** bought
7 hammer	**8** thousand	**9** thought
10 caught	**11** straw	**12** butter
13 table	**14** salad	**15** crawl

Review: Schwa; Vowel Variant: /ô/aw, au(gh), ou(gh)

Phonics Practice Book

Harcourt Brace School Publishers

Name _____

Use the rhyming words to complete the poem. Then answer the questions.

caught	stronger	thought	able
taught	ago	crawl	

1. Have you ever heard the fable about the turtle who was

   _____able_____?

2. Very, very long _____ago_____, Turtle and Hare's race was

   the show.

3. Hare said speediness can't be _____taught_____, can't be

   promised, and it can't be bought.

4. But Turtle did not give up at all and moved along at a steady

   _____crawl_____.

5. "Since I have time, I think I ought to take a nap right here,"

   Hare _____thought_____.

6. Turtle kept it up much longer and proved that he was really

   _____stronger_____.

7. In the end, Hare had been taught that Turtle now could not be

   _____caught_____!

Review: Schwa; Vowel Variant: /ô/ *aw, au(gh), ou(gh)*

Circle the word that names the picture. Then write the word.

1 (beard) beast bread — *beard*	**2** chair (cheer) chore — *cheer*	**3** suit soon (soup) — *soup*
4 mean main (moon) — *moon*	**5** chain cheer (chair) — *chair*	**6** (table) tickle towel — *table*
7 peer (pear) people — *pear*	**8** (straw) stream stray — *straw*	**9** sought squirm (square) — *square*
10 cut (caught) couple — *caught*	**11** (fruit) fry fright — *fruit*	**12** boot bite (bought) — *bought*
13 flea (flew) flow — *flew*	**14** (butter) battle button — *butter*	**15** glow (glue) group — *glue*

Cumulative Review: /ir/*ear, eer*; /âr/*air, ear, are*;
/oo/*ue, ew, oo, ou, ui*; /ə/*a*, /əl/*le*, /ər/*er*; /ô/*aw, au(gh), ou(gh)*

Harcourt Brace School Publishers

Phonics Practice Book

Look at the picture. Then follow the directions.

We Care About Deer is written on one poster.

1. Write *We Care About Deer* at the top of one poster.
2. Draw an arrow pointing to the person who taught the class about animals. arrow pointing to the teacher
3. Draw a zebra on another poster. a zebra is drawn on one poster
4. Draw a jar of glue on a desk. jar of glue drawn on desk
5. Draw a bicycle on the playground. bicycle is drawn on playground
6. Write the year in the date on the board. year is written after date on board
7. Draw a few more fish in the tank.
   a few fish are drawn in fish tank

Cumulative Review of /ir/*ear, eer;* /âr/*air, ear, are;*
/o͞o/*ue, ew, oo, ou, ui;* /ə/*a,* /əl/ *le,* /ər/*er;* /ô/*aw, au(gh), ou(gh)*

Fill in the circle next to the word that names the picture.

1			
○ thunder	○ dare	● crawl	○ glow
● table	○ door	○ caught	○ good
○ tear	● deer	○ cough	● glue

5	6	7	8
○ bar	○ chop	● salad	○ skip
● bear	● chair	○ sled	○ squid
○ bead	○ cheer	○ sleet	● square

9	10	11	12
○ tight	● water	○ hare	● thousand
● taught	○ waddle	○ hire	○ thought
○ tooth	○ whistle	● hear	○ taught

13	14	15	16
○ jungle	○ sports	○ seat	○ threat
● jewel	○ spoke	● suit	○ thought
○ jacket	● spoon	○ sight	○ those

Test: /ir/*ear, eer;* /âr/*air, ear, are;*
/o͞o/*ue, ew, oo, ou, ui;* /ə/*a,* /əl/*le,* /ər/*er;* /ô/*aw, au(gh), ou(gh)*

Harcourt Brace School Publishers

Name _____

Fill in the circle next to the sentence that tells about the picture.

1
- ○ The children wish they could get into the water.
- ○ The children wish they could use a hammer.
- ○ The children wish they could read a letter.

2
- ○ They fear the water.
- ● They get their gear.
- ○ They look under the car.

3
- ● They thought the sky was clear and blue, but then they saw clouds.
- ○ They saw a hawk in the clear blue sky.
- ○ They caught sight of a plane in the clear, blue sky.

4
- ● The wind blew their hair.
- ○ The wind blew over a chair.
- ○ The wind did not blow.

5
- ○ They got caught in a river.
- ● They got caught in a rain shower.
- ○ They were taught how to swim.

6
- ○ They were dry because they wore their coats.
- ● They got wet, though not in the pool.
- ○ They got wet at school.

7
- ● They agreed to wait for a while.
- ○ They were able to swim in the water.
- ○ They agreed to put a puzzle together.

8
- ● The children gave a cheer when the sun came out.
- ○ The children did not care when the sun came out.
- ○ The children stood on chairs when the sun came out.

Phonics Practice Book

Test: /ir/*ear, eer*; /âr/*air, ear, are*;
/o͞o/*ue, ew, oo, ou, ui*; /ə/*a*, /əl/*le*, /ər/*er*; /ô/*aw, au(gh), ou(gh)*

181

Name _____

 snail   **smile**   **scoop**

When two consonants come together in a word, you usually blend together the sounds they stand for. Write the word that names the picture.

scout	scarf	snow	scale
smock	smoke	scarecrow	sneaker
snout	snake	score	smile

1. scarf
2. smock
3. snake
4. scarecrow
5. snow
6. smoke
7. score
8. sneaker
9. smile
10. scale
11. snout
12. scout

Name _____

<u>st</u>amp   **<u>sk</u>ate**   **<u>sp</u>oon**

Answer each question with a word that begins with *st, sk,* or *sp*.

1. What belongs on a letter and rhymes with *damp*? _____ stamp _____

2. What has eight legs and rhymes with *rider*? _____ spider _____

3. What do you see when you go outside and look up? It rhymes with *fly*.

   _____ sky _____

4. What do clowns walk on to look very tall? They rhyme with *tilts*.

   _____ stilts _____

5. What covers your body and rhymes with *tin*? _____ skin _____

6. What means "to begin" and rhymes with *part*? _____ start _____

7. What animal gives off a strong smell and rhymes with *bunk*?

   _____ skunk _____

8. What do you walk up to go from the first floor to the second floor? It

   rhymes with *chairs.* _____ stairs _____

9. What can a toy top do? It rhymes with *tin*. _____ spin _____

10. What is another name for a small rock? It rhymes with *bone*.

    _____ stone _____

bread **crab** **grapes** **frog** **dragon** **train** **pretzel**

Circle the word that names the picture. Then write the word.

1		2		3	
	foot		rib		fries
	(fruit)		club		rise
	flute		(crib)		(prize)
	fruit		crib		prize

4		5		6	
	trim		boom		(grill)
	(drum)		(broom)		girl
	damp		room		rail
	drum		broom		grill

7		8		9	
	tea		(princess)		farm
	(tree)		rinse		crane
	free		pinch		(frame)
	tree		princess		frame

10		11		12	
	desk		tuck		rush
	(dress)		rack		(brush)
	fresh		(truck)		bush
	dress		truck		brush

13		14		15	
	raft		row		dill
	gas		cow		(drill)
	(grass)		(crow)		roll
	grass		crow		drill

Initial Clusters with *r*

Phonics Practice Book

Harcourt Brace School Publishers

The words below are in the puzzle. Some words go down and some words go across. Find and circle each one.

branch	crab	grill	crown	pretzel
brush	cry	dragon	train	prize

P	R	E	T	Z	E	L	B
R	Y	C	R	O	W	N	R
I	D	R	A	G	O	N	A
Z	G	R	I	L	L	Z	N
E	R	X	N	C	R	Y	C
C	R	A	B	R	U	S	H

Write the word from the puzzle that names each picture.

1. branch
2. brush
3. crab
4. crown
5. cry
6. dragon
7. grill
8. pretzel
9. prize
10. train

When two consonants come together in a word, you usually blend together the sounds they stand for. Write the letters that complete each picture name.

blocks   **clover**   **planet**   **flag**

1. c‍l ock	2. fl ag	3. pl um
4. bl ouse	5. fl y	6. pl ate
7. fl ame	8. bl anket	9. c‍l oud
10. cl am	11. pl ug	12. bl ack

Follow the directions below the picture.

1. Circle the club member who is climbing the ladder.

   boy is circled

2. Write *Club* on the sign over the door.

   Club written on sign

3. Draw a pretty blossom on the tree.

   blossom drawn on tree

4. Add a smoke trail behind the plane that is flying in the sky.

   smoke trail drawn behind plane in sky

5. Draw blinds on the window.

   blinds drawn on window

6. Draw a fluffy cloud over the sun in the sky.

   cloud drawn in sky

7. Draw a flag on top of the roof.

   flag drawn on roof

8. Circle the pail of plums on the floor.

   pail of plums circled

9. Draw a folded blanket on the porch.

   blanket drawn on porch

Initial Clusters with *l*   187

swan

twins

Circle the word that names the picture.
Write the word on the line.

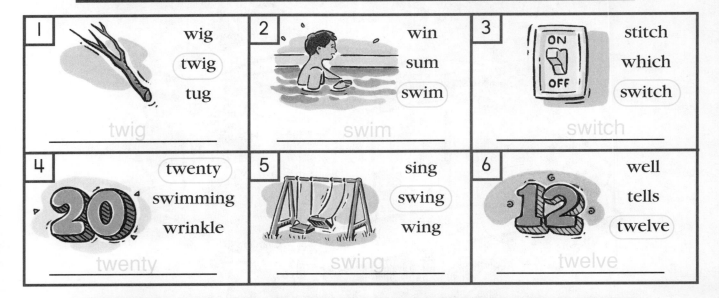

1	wig	2	win	3	stitch
	(twig)		sum		which
	tug		(swim)		(switch)
	twig		_swim_		_switch_

4	(twenty)	5	sing	6	well
	swimming		(swing)		tells
	wrinkle		wing		(twelve)
	twenty		_swing_		_twelve_

Write the word that completes each sentence. You will not use all the words.

swam	twice	twinkle	twin
tweet	sweater	sweep	sweet

7. Kim likes to eat _____ _sweet_ _____ apples.

8. Fred's pet bird can only say, "_____ _tweet_ _____."

9. Sue looks just like her _____ _twin_ _____ sister.

10. On cool days Joe wears a _____ _sweater_ _____.

11. Will you help me _____ _sweep_ _____ the floor?

12. Ruth went to the zoo _____ _twice_ _____ last week.

Initial Clusters with *w*

Phonics Practice Book

Harcourt Brace School Publishers

Name _____

Write the word that begins with *sw* or *tw* that answers each question.

1. What means "very fast" and rhymes with *lift*? _____ swift

2. What is a way to clean up that rhymes with *creep*? _____ sweep

3. What sound from a bird rhymes with *feet*? _____ tweet

4. What means "more than once" and rhymes with *nice*? _____ twice

5. What is something on a playground that rhymes with *king*?

    _____ swing

6. What might a dancer do that rhymes with *girl*? _____ twirl

7. What turns things on and off and rhymes with *ditch*? _____ switch

8. What do you call sisters or brothers born at the same time? It rhymes

    with *pins*. _____ twins

9. What do you do to a jar lid that rhymes with *wrist*? _____ twist

10. What way to move in water rhymes with *him*? _____ swim

11. What is ten plus ten? It rhymes with *plenty*. _____ twenty

12. What word tells how honey tastes? It rhymes with *street*. _____ sweet

Harcourt Brace School Publishers

Write the letters that complete each picture name.

1	2	3
sm ile	pl um	cr ab

4	5	6
sp ider	br oom	sw im

7	8	9
bl ocks	sn ow	tw ig

10	11	12
fl ute	tr ain	st amp

13	14	15
dr um	cl am	sk unk

Read the story and answer the questions.

"SNOW DAYS"

Snow flurries started to fall early on Tuesday. Soon snowflakes covered everything. We were pleased when our teacher sent us home early. We were not scared of a little snow.

"Hooray!" we yelled as we skidded home on the ice.

At first we just watched the blizzard from the window. The sparkling snow looked so pretty.

On Wednesday the snow was still blowing around. It piled in drifts in front of the door. We could not even clean off the sidewalk. When we opened the door, a blast of swirling snow blew in. The schools were closed. We watched some TV. Then we played some games. Our first snow day had been fun. But by Wednesday evening we felt a little bored.

On Thursday we were just plain crabby. We were tired of snowflakes swirling and twirling. They did not look pretty any more. We were tired of freezing breezes blowing around us. We were tired of being closed up in the house.

On Friday morning the bright sun climbed into a blue sky. No more blizzard! We felt free. We all smiled. Believe it or not, it felt great to be going back to school. We could not wait to see our friends.

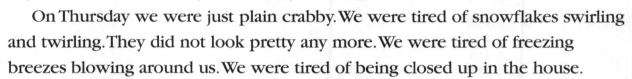
Possible responses are shown.

1. How did the children feel about the snow on Tuesday?

   They were happy.
   _____

2. How did the children feel when it was time to go back to school? Why?

   They were happy. They wanted to get out
   _____

   of the house and see their friends.
   _____

Harcourt Brace School Publishers

scratch   **strawberry**   **spray**   **squirrel**

Write the word from the box that answers each question.

square   stream   spring   scrub   string   street   strike
scrap   scream   stranger   squid   spread

1. What is a season of the year? _____spring_____

2. What is something you do to a dirty floor? _____scrub_____

3. What word for a little river rhymes with *team*? _____stream_____

4. What is a place for driving cars? _____street_____

5. What is something you tie onto a kite? _____string_____

6. What is a shape that rhymes with *rare*? _____square_____

7. What is something left over that rhymes with *map*?

_____scrap_____

8. Who is a person you do not know? _____stranger_____

9. What is something you can do with jelly? It rhymes with *head*.

_____spread_____

10. What is a sea animal that rhymes with *lid*? _____squid_____

11. What is a word for a loud yell? _____scream_____

12. What word means "a swing that misses the ball"? _____strike_____

Circle the word that completes the sentence. Write the word on the line.

1

spring
ring
string

It is a warm day in spring _____ .

2

scrapbooks
scatter
strawberries

Casey plants strawberries _____ .

3

scrapes
soaps
straps

First she scrapes _____ away the weeds.

4

pouts
spots
sprouts

Then she plants the sprouts _____ in the ground.

5

sports
squirts
spreads

She squirts _____ water on the new plants.

6

straw
trees
saw

She covers them with straw _____ .

7

sting
song
string

She makes a fence with string _____ .

8

strap
scrub
sub

She will scrub _____ her hands before she eats the berries.

Initial Clusters: *scr, str, spr, squ*

193

Name _____

Follow the directions. Write the new word. Then draw a picture of it.

1	Start with *wash*. Change *w* to *squ*.	squash	Drawings will vary.
2	Start with *wipe*. Change *w* to *str*.	stripe	
3	Start with *green*. Change the *gr* to *scr*.	screen	
4	Start with *hare*. Change *h* to *squ*.	square	
5	Start with *sing*. Change *s* to *spr*.	spring	
6	Start with *bring*. Change *br* to *str*.	string	

Initial Clusters: *scr, str, spr, squ*

Phonics Practice Book

Harcourt Brace School Publishers

Name _____

The Big Game

We sprint to the field.
The crowd gives a scream.
We are strong, we are mighty—
The number one team.

We spring up so high
To catch every ball.
We watch the other team—
Squirm, squeal, and sprawl.

By the end of the game,
We're scruffy and dirty,
But we feel no stress—
The score is zero to thirty.

Bright streamers are flying.
Winning is fun!
We've stretched out our streak
And are still number ONE!

Possible responses are shown.

1. How do the players feel at the end of the game? Why?
   They are happy because they are still number one.

2. Write a headline about the game for the team scrapbook.
   Responses will vary. Possible answer is: Number one team wins again!

Harcourt Brace School Publishers

ne<u>st</u>

pa<u>int</u>

be<u>lt</u>

gi<u>ft</u>

Write the word that completes each sentence.

| adult | best | breakfast | cent | cost | elephant |
| feast | gift | hunt | rent | just | want |

1. I _____want_____ you to come to my birthday party.

2. Eat only a small _____breakfast_____ in the morning.

3. Lunch will be a real _____feast_____ !

4. After lunch we will _____hunt_____ for hidden prizes.

5. You might want to _____rent_____ or make a costume.

6. Joe wants to make an _____elephant_____ costume.

7. I think that will _____cost_____ too much.

8. I do not want to spend one _____cent_____ .

9. I might _____just_____ come as a mouse.

10. Tell your mom that an _____adult_____ will be in charge.

11. We will have the _____best_____ time ever!

12. Oh, I almost forgot. Do not bring a birthday _____gift_____ .

Final Clusters with *t: st, nt, lt, ft*

Phonics Practice Book

Circle the word that fits the clue.

1. You eat this in the morning.
   bolt   (breakfast)   bent

2. This can be used to lock your door.
   bush   (bolt)   ball

3. You do this with a pencil to make letters or words.
   pest   prize   (print)

4. This means a pile of snow blown by the wind.
   drill   (drift)   dent

5. This is a horse's baby.
   cold   (colt)   cart

6. This means "the land next to an ocean."
   (coast)   coat   cone

7. This is the opposite of right.
   list   laugh   (left)

8. This often goes with pepper.
   sift   sail   (salt)

9. This has a trunk but never packs it.
   eleven   telephone   (elephant)

10. You may do this to a cake after you bake it.
    (frost)   fish   flat

11. This is something you might float on in a lake.
    (raft)   rent   roof

12. This is not the back.
    from   (front)   frog

Name_____

1

ju mp

2

ha nd

3

sta mp

4

mi lk

5

ba nd

6

de sk

7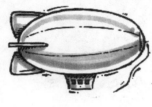

bli mp

8

chi ld

9

ca mp

10

po nd

11

du mp

12

ma sk

13

sa nd

14

wa sp

15

ra mp

Final Clusters: *lk, sk, sp, ld, mp, nd*

Phonics Practice Book

Name _____

Come to the Farm!

Are you tired of sitting at a desk all day? Then spend this summer at the Romp family's farm. See what it is like to work on the land.

You will be outside in the brisk, crisp air all day. You can work in the field with Mr. Romp. You can husk corn or milk a cow in the barn. You can pull a clump of weeds or pick plump, ripe apples in the orchard. You can join in on any household task you like. Do not be afraid to ask questions. By the end of your stay, you will understand how a farm really works.

When each day's work is done, it is time to have some fun. You can attend a band concert in town or swim in the pond. You can look for wild animal tracks in the woods. You may even make a new friend or two.

Write the answers to the questions.

Possible responses are shown.

1. Where is a good place to spend the summer?

   the Romp family's farm

2. What task can you do in the barn? You can milk a cow.

3. What task can you do in the orchard?

   You can pick plump, ripe apples.

4. Where can you swim after the work is done?

   in the pond

REVIEW | **Write the word that completes each sentence.**

> cold   colt   dent   desk   elk   left
> raft   scrap   string   stripe   toast   wasp

1. Jane had orange juice, _____ toast _____, and cereal for breakfast.

2. A baby horse is called a _____ colt _____.

3. The _____ elk _____ has large antlers.

4. Be careful. The _____ wasp _____ may sting!

5. Leroy likes to float on a _____ raft _____ in his pool.

6. The art teacher made a puppet from a _____ scrap _____ of cloth.

7. We tied a _____ string _____ to the kite.

8. A skunk has a _____ stripe _____ on its back.

9. The computer is on the _____ desk _____.

10. Turn _____ left _____ at the next street.

11. The car has a _____ dent _____ on the side.

12. It is too _____ cold _____ to swim.

Harcourt Brace School Publishers

Circle the word that completes the sentence. Write the word on the line.

1	The squid lives in the ___cold___ waters of the ocean.	coal call (cold)
2	The squid can ___squirt___ a jet of water from its head.	scrap sit (squirt)
3	The jet makes it ___spring___ through the water.	soap (spring) sit
4	It jets around to ___hunt___ for food.	(hunt) hut him
5	The squid has ten arms but not one ___hand___.	hen had (hand)
6	A squid squirts ink to hide in so its enemies can't ___find___ it.	fall (find) fill
7	It can ___drift___ away inside its cloud of ink.	dot date (drift)

city

cow

When *c* is followed by *e, i,* or *y,* the *c* usually stands for the sound at the beginning of *city*. When *c* is followed by other letters, it usually stands for the sound at the beginning of *cow*.
Write the word that names each picture.

cents	center	cereal	computer
camera	corn	cabin	cymbal
celery	camel	comb	ceiling

1 cereal	2 cabin	3 center
4 computer	5 corn	6 camera
7 cymbal	8 cents	9 ceiling
10 comb	11 camel	12 celery

Initial Hard and Soft *c*

Phonics Practice Book

Circle the soft *c* word that best finishes each sentence. Write it on the line.

1	Welcome to Centerville A Good Place to Live	Centerville will __celebrate__ its centennial.	(celebrate) enjoying calling
2		This means that the __city__ is 100 years old.	candy town (city)
3		Centerville is __certain__ to have a big party.	contain (certain) sure
4		The __citizens__ will get together.	people cousins (citizens)
5		They will come to the __center__ of town.	(center) candle middle
6		A __celebrity__ will make a speech.	calendar (celebrity) star

Harcourt Brace School Publishers

Name _____

Write the hard *c* words to complete the rhyme.

cackle	cat	cocoon	cold
colt	couch	cover	cow

When the leaves turn gold, and the days grow _____ cold _____ ,

When wood fires crackle, and starlings _____ cackle _____ ,

Animals may discover it is time to take _____ cover _____ .

Caterpillar will sleep soon in its warm _____ cocoon _____ .

Mouse will say, "Ouch!" and hide under the _____ couch _____ .

"To the barn I must bolt," says the frisky _____ colt _____ .

"Where is my green grass now?" complains the _____ cow _____ .

"I will lie here and grow fat," purrs the warm, cozy _____ cat _____ .

Write the answers to the questions.

Possible responses are shown.

1. What season is the poem about?

fall or autumn

_____

2. Why do the animals need to take cover?

because it is getting cold outside

_____

Harcourt Brace School Publishers

Read the story, and answer the questions.

Cooking Up Trouble

Cindy loves to cook. So does her brother, Carl. One day they got out their old cookbook. They looked at the recipes— Celery Salad, Country Ham, Corn on the Cob, and Candied Yams.

"Ugh!" said Carl. "We have tried every recipe here. This cookbook is boring."

"You are certainly right!" answered Cindy. "I have an idea. We can make something new. We can make up our own cookbook."

So they did. Here is the table of contents for their new cookbook:

Cucumber Candy l	Cement Cookies 5
Centipede Stew 2	Cedar Cereal 6

1. What recipes were in the old cookbook?

   Celery Salad, Country Ham, Corn on the Cob, Candied Yams

2. Why did the children make a new cookbook?

   Their old cookbook was boring. They had already

   tried every recipe in it.

3. Which of the new recipes would you be willing to try?

   Responses will vary.

Name _____

Circle the word that names each picture. Then write the word.

1		2		3	
	package (palace) parka *palace*		fender fork (fence) *fence*		itchy inch (icy) *icy*

4		5		6	
	(fancy) flock fiction *fancy*		(piece) pack pets *piece*		polite (police) pails *police*

7		8		9	
	mike (mice) music *mice*		rack rust (race) *race*		(juice) jacket join *juice*

10		11		12	
	(space) speak sports *space*		lake (lace) lack *lace*		slide (slice) slick *slice*

13		14		15	
	bound bow (bounce) *bounce*		praise (price) press *price*		(face) fact fair *face*

Harcourt Brace School Publishers

Name _____

1. Draw a box of supplies in the canoe.
   box of supplies drawn in the canoe

2. Write *Camp Cardinal* on the sign.
   Camp Cardinal written on the sign

3. Find a word that means "money" and circle it.
   cents circled

4. Draw smoke coming from the cabin's chimney.
   smoke coming from the chimney

5. Mark an X on the candle and cup on the picnic table.
   the candle and cup marked with an X

6. Circle the cat in the window.
   the cat in the window circled

7. Draw logs for the cabin walls.
   logs drawn on the cabin walls

8. Mark an X in the center of the door.
   center of the door marked with an X

9. Draw some corn on the cob on the plate.
   corn on the cob drawn on the plate

10. Add some buttons to the camper's coat.
    buttons drawn on the camper's coat

Now circle each soft *c* word and underline each hard *c* word in the directions.

Harcourt Brace School Publishers

When *g* is followed by *e, y,* or *i*, it often stands for the soft sound heard at the beginning of *gem*. When *g* is followed by other letters, it usually stands for the hard sound heard at the beginning of *golf*.

Write the word that names each picture. You will not use all the words.

gem

golf

gift	gym	girl	gem	giraffe	goose	gull	goat
garden	game	gymnast	giant	goose gerbil	gum	gorilla

1	2	3
gerbil	gymnast	game

4	5	6
giant	goose	gym

7	8	9
gum	garden	goat

10	11	12
gull	giraffe	gorilla

Name _____

Circle the soft *g* word that completes each sentence. Then write the word on the line.

1	My friend is a very good _gymnast_ .	gentleman (gymnast) jumper
2	She is not tall, but she leaps as high as a _giant_ would.	germ pony (giant)
3	Every _gesture_ she makes is graceful.	general movement (gesture)
4	When she performs in meets, she sparkles like a _gem_ .	center (gem) general
5	Sometimes I visit the _gym_ with her.	(gym) gentle mall
6	My friend is so small that next to her, I feel like a _giraffe_ !	tumbler gym (giraffe)

Phonics Practice Book   Hard and Soft *g*   209

Write the hard _g_ word that completes each rhyme.

> Gail   gallery   gas   gate
> goat   gobble   gorilla   guppy

1. A purple raincoat

   Would look odd on a ___goat___.

2. When you need to pass,

   Just step on the ___gas___.

3. A painting by Valerie

   Hangs in the art ___gallery___.

4. I asked for a puppy.

   Mom got me a ___guppy___.

5. Turkeys walk with a wobble.

   Then they stop and say "___gobble___."

6. The sailor told a tale

   Of a pale whale named ___Gail___.

7. If you plan to be late,

   We won't lock the ___gate___.

8. "Chocolate or vanilla?"

   Sam asked the ___gorilla___.

Read the story, and answer the questions.

Gentle Ginger

Ginger is a pretty dog. She got her name because she is a golden retriever. Many dogs just gulp down their meals and play games all day, but not Ginger. She goes to school. When she finishes school, she will go to live with Gina, who uses a wheelchair. She will help out in her new home.

At first, school was hard for Ginger. She had to learn many commands and gestures. She learned to get things for Gina and even how to open a gate. She was taught to be gentle and not to gallop around while she was working.

Now Ginger lives with Gina. Gina thinks Ginger is a genius. But Gina is good at learning, too. She has learned how to make work seem like a game to Ginger. The best part is that Gina and Ginger are good friends.

Possible responses are shown.

1. How did Ginger learn to help Gina?

Ginger went to school.
_____

2. Name two things Ginger does to help Gina.

Ginger gets things for Gina and can open the gate.
_____

3. What does Gina think of Ginger?

Gina thinks Ginger is a genius; they are good friends.
_____

Circle the word that names each picture. Then write the word.

1. jug / **judge** / jade — judge	2. stag / stake / **stage** — stage	3. **cottage** / coating / cooking — cottage
4. **bridge** / brag / bread — bridge	5. pig / **page** / pogo — page	6. cling / **cage** / cart — cage
7. lucky / **luggage** / leg — luggage	8. **badge** / bag / bad — badge	9. cutting / carving / **cabbage** — cabbage
10. fry / **fudge** / fad — fudge	11. **dodge** / dog / did — dodge	12. voting / violin / **village** — village

Harcourt Brace School Publishers

Name _____

1. Write *Pets to Go* on the sign.

   Pets to Go written on the sign

2. Draw two goldfish in the aquarium.

   two goldfish drawn in the aquarium

3. Draw a cage around the bird.

   cage drawn around the little bird

4. Add a name badge to the sales clerk's shirt.

   name badge drawn on the sales clerk's shirt

5. Draw a gate on the gerbils' pen.

   gate drawn on the gerbils' pen

6. Circle the picture of the goat.

   the picture of the goat is circled

7. Draw a hat on the goose.

   hat drawn on the goose

8. Mark an X on the animal that does not belong in a pet store.

   the giraffe and/or goat is marked with an X

Now circle each soft *g* word and underline each hard *g* word in the directions.

Harcourt Brace School Publishers

REVIEW **Find the words that fit the clues. Write the words in the puzzle.**

giggle　center　citrus　cage　gas　giraffe
page　giant　fence　edge　goat　icy　go

ACROSS
1. The middle part
2. Laugh
6. Huge
7. A part of a book
9. Something that divides two back yards
10. Fuel for a car

DOWN
1. Safe home for some kinds of pets
2. An animal with a very long neck
3. The rim
4. An animal with a beard
5. A kind of fruit
8. Frozen
10. The opposite of *stop*

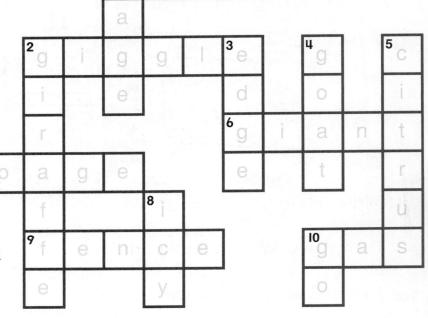

Harcourt Brace School Publishers

Circle the word that answers each riddle. Then write the word.

REVIEW

1. We are tiny rodents that scurry and squeak. We are _____mice_____.

   make   (mice)   mug

2. I do not like to brag, but I am very, very smart. I am a _____genius_____.

   (genius)   canes   gentle

3. I am a bed, but I do not have pillows or blankets. I am a home for

   flowers. I am a _____garden_____.

   carton   gerbil   (garden)

4. I am not a boy. I am a _____girl_____.

   grill   curl   (girl)

5. I say "honk, honk," but I do not have a horn. I am a _____goose_____.

   (goose)   cost   gas

6. I am shaped like a star. A sheriff may wear me. I am a _____badge_____.

   back   (badge)   beg

7. I seem very big to you. To me, you look small. I am a _____giant_____.

   game   (giant)   icing

8. I work in a courtroom. I decide who is right and who is wrong.

   I am a _____judge_____.

   jug   goat   (judge)

9. I am a small wooden bird. I live in a clock. I am a _____cuckoo_____.

   pogo   (cuckoo)   kicker

10. My name sounds like a country for automobiles. But I am really a flower.

    I am a _____carnation_____.

    garden   certain   (carnation)

Name _____

Circle the word that names the picture.

1. foot / food / (flute)

2. slim / (swim) / same

3. digging / wagon / (dragon)

4. (cloud) / could / cold

5. (tree) / tee / tear

6. soup / (scoop) / coop

7. late / slate / (plate)

8. rise / (prize) / freeze

9. neck / (snake) / soak

Write one of the words that you circled above to complete each sentence. You will not use all of the words.

10. Would you like a _____scoop_____ of ice cream?

11. A _____dragon_____ is found only in fairy tales.

12. The _____snake_____ curled up on a rock in the sun.

13. Terry's goat won first _____prize_____ at the fair.

14. Will Trina play a song on her _____flute_____?

15. There was not one _____cloud_____ in the blue sky.

Name_____

Write each word under the correct heading.

adult   cow   girl   skunk   twins   camp   crab
giraffe   squid   village   child   fly   judge
street   wasp   city   garden   pond   student

People	Places	Animals
adult	camp	giraffe
child	city	cow
girl	garden	crab
judge	pond	fly
student	street	skunk
twins	village	squid
		wasp

Fill in the circle next to the letters that complete each picture name. Then write the letters.

1. ○ gr ● sm ○ sn — **sm**oke	2. ○ sk ○ nd ● ft — gi**ft**	3. ● fr ○ tr ○ tw — **fr**uit
4. ○ sk ○ scr ● squ — **squ**are	5. ● bl ○ cl ○ dr — **bl**ock	6. ○ lt ● mp ○ sp — sta**mp**
7. ● fl ○ fr ○ bl — **fl**y	8. ○ sn ● sk ○ spr — **sk**unk	9. ○ bl ○ gr ● tr — **tr**uck
10. ○ sc ○ cl ● cr — **cr**ib	11. ○ mp ● nt ○ lk — ce**nt**	12. ● st ○ sn ○ squ — **st**ar
13. ○ sp ● pr ○ fl — **pr**etzel	14. ● lt ○ ft ○ nd — sa**lt**	15. ○ sw ○ str ● tw — **tw**ins

Test: Consonant Clusters, Hard and Soft *c* and *g*

Fill in the circle next to the sentence that tells about the picture.

CHECK-UP

1.
- ○ I love my home in the city.
- ○ It is good to live in a cave.
- ○ A tree house makes a good home.

2.
- ○ My suitcase is too big to lift now.
- ○ I like to ride my bike.
- ○ I am going on a trip to the country.

3.
- ○ A ride on my bike is great.
- ○ A hike in the forest is fun.
- ○ A walk down the street is exciting.

4.
- ○ I think I see a lion.
- ○ I think I spot an elk.
- ○ I think I see a cat.

5.
- ○ Birds swoop through the branches.
- ○ Twelve bears march past the trees.
- ○ A little skunk hides in the brush.

6.
- ○ A monkey swings on the vines.
- ○ A woodpecker drums on a tree trunk.
- ○ A crow sits on a nest.

7.
- ○ The wind makes waves on the sea.
- ○ Cars drive down the road.
- ○ The stream runs over the rocks.

8.
- ○ The lawn is brown and dry.
- ○ Grasshoppers cover the path.
- ○ Wildflowers grow on the lawn.

church

Choose the word that names the picture. Write the word on the line. You will not use all of the words.

| chimney | chat | chick | cherry | chair |
| carry | | cheese | | chain |

1. chair

2. chick

3. chimney

4. cheese

5. cherry

6. chain

Complete each sentence by writing a *ch* word from the boxes above.

7. In winter, I like to sit in my _____chair_____ by the fire.

8. Mom closes the door and locks it with the _____chain_____.

9. It is nice to see the smoke go up the _____chimney_____.

10. Dad grills a _____cheese_____ sandwich on the stove.

11. Then I have a dish of fruit with a _____cherry_____ on top.

12. I feel as snug as a _____chick_____ inside its nest.

wa<u>tch</u>

 lun<u>ch</u>

Write the word that names each picture.
You will not use all of the words.

patch	hatch	brush	punch	sandwich
torch	inch	pitch	peach	catch
watch	branch	stitch	church	itch

1	2	3
patch	branch	peach

4	5	6
torch	hatch	church

7	8	9
itch	sandwich	pitch

10	11	12
catch	inch	punch

Digraph: Final /ch/ *ch, tch*

bru<u>sh</u>

Write the word from the box that answers each clue.

sheep	shell	cash	shop	shrimp
dish	shut	hush	ship	shrink

1. It begins like *shark* and rhymes with *deep*. It is a kind of animal.

   What is it? _____ sheep

2. It begins like *cab* and rhymes with *mash*. When you have it, you can save it

   or spend it. What is it? _____ cash

3. It begins like *hum* and rhymes with *brush*. You say it to stop a noise.

   What is it? _____ hush

4. It begins like *shrub* and rhymes with *drink*. It happens when something

   gets smaller. What is it? _____ shrink

5. It begins like *shark* and rhymes with *stop*. You do it in a store.

   What is it? _____ shop

6. It begins like *shark* and rhymes with *well*. You might find one by the sea.

   What is it? _____ shell

7. It begins like *shark* and ends like *zip*. It is something that floats in the sea.

   What is it? _____ ship

8. It begins like *did* and rhymes with *fish*. It is another word for *plate*.

   What is it? dish _____

9. It begins like *shark* and rhymes with *cut*. You do it to a door to close it.

   What is it? _____ shut

10. It begins like *shrub* and rhymes with *blimp*. It is a small sea animal.

   What is it? _____ shrimp

Digraphs: Initial and Final /sh/*sh*; Initial /shr/*shr*

Harcourt Brace School Publishers

Name _____

Choose the word that fits each clue. Write the words in the puzzle.

| rush | shrink | brush | shore | sheep |
| fish | shark | shake | shrub | shorts |

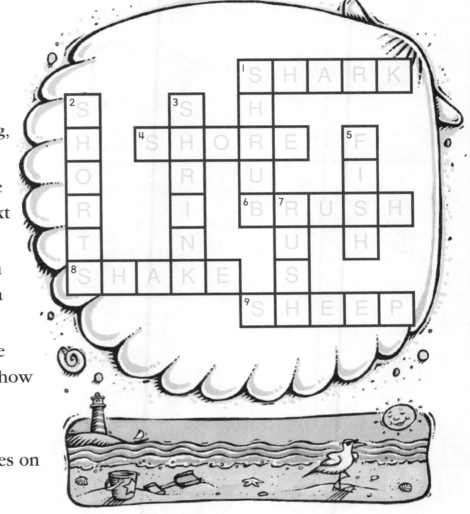

ACROSS

1. A large sea animal with big, sharp teeth

4. The part of the land that is next to the sea

6. Something you need to paint a picture

8. How you move your head to show "no"

9. A white, fluffy animal that lives on a farm

DOWN

1. Another word for *bush*

2. Something you may wear outdoors on a warm day

3. What some things do when they get wet

5. An animal you can catch with a worm and a hook

7. How you move when you are in a hurry

Digraph: Initial and Final /sh/*sh*; Initial Cluster: /shr/*shr*

Name _____

  3

thumb   **tooth**   **three**

Write the word that names each picture. You will not use all of the words.

thermos	path	three	throne	thorn	thirteen	moth	mouth
bath	tooth	thimble	throat	think	thief	thread	thirty

1 thorn	**2** tooth	**3** thimble
4 thirteen	**5** thermos	**6** throne
7 thread	**8** throat	**9** moth
10 path	**11** bath	**12** thirty
13 mouth	**14** three	**15** thief

Digraphs: Initial and Final /th/*th*; Initial /thr/*thr*

Phonics Practice Book

Harcourt Brace School Publishers

Name _____

> **Read the page from Michael's diary. Then use a _th_ or _thr_ word from the diary to complete each sentence below.**

Dear Diary,

    Guess what I did last Thursday. I went on my first roller-coaster ride! I got in line three times. Each time I got out of line to think it over. I was scared to death. The fourth time I stayed in line. My heart was thumping.

    I hung on tight as the cart went up the hill. "This is a stupid thing to do," I thought. The ride up the first hill lasted about thirteen seconds. My teeth began to chatter. My head started to throb, and my heart started to thump. We went over the big hill.

    The drop down took my breath away. Then I saw that the ride was smooth. It was the biggest thrill of my life. The seat felt like a throne. "This is fun!" I yelled. Now I cannot wait to go again. I could ride a thousand more times.

    And that is the truth!

1. Michael rode the roller coaster last _____Thursday_____.

2. He was scared to _____death_____.

3. He felt like a king on a _____throne_____.

4. The ride was fast but _____smooth_____.

5. Now he wants to go back a _____thousand_____ times.

Digraphs: Initial and Final /th/*th* ; Initial /thr/*thr*
• Reading Words in Context

whale

Say each picture name. Write *wh* if the picture name begins with the sound you hear at the beginning of *whale*.

1. ____wh____iskers

2. _____eese

3. ____wh____istle

4. ____wh____isper

5. ____wh____eel

6. ____wh____ite

Choose the word that completes each sentence. Write the word on the line.

(wheat   when   what   why   where)

7. ____What____ time do you wake up in the morning?

8. I wake up ____when____ my alarm goes off.

9. I know ____why____ I have to get up early.

10. I have to catch the school bus. The bus driver knows ____where____ I live.

11. Mom packs me a cheese sandwich on whole ____wheat____ bread for my lunch.

Harcourt Brace School Publishers

The words below are hidden in the puzzle. Some words go across. Some words go down. Find and circle each one.

wheat   whistle   whale   wheel   whiskers   whisper

W	H	E	E	L	Z	W	L	R	F	U	W
H	W	H	A	L	E	T	S	L	N	A	H
E	B	G	W	H	I	S	K	E	R	S	I
A	C	W	H	I	S	P	E	R	J	Y	S
T	V	J	I	R	L	X	I	Z	D	V	T
M	K	M	X	U	I	T	B	L	E	Q	L
A	D	R	E	B	X	I	S	K	G	L	E

Write the word from the puzzle that names each picture.

1 whale	2 wheel	3 wheat
4 whistle	5 whiskers	6 whisper

Harcourt Brace School Publishers

SUPER REVIEW

Say each picture name. Write the letters that complete each word.

1	2	3	4
__thr__ ee	__th__ umb	__sh__ ip	__wh__ eel
5	6	7	8
__ch__ ain	__th__ orn	__thr__ one	fi __sh__
9	10	11	12
__wh__ ale	__shr__ imp	__ch__ air	__thr__ ow
13	14	15	16
__sh__ eep	tee __th__	ben __ch__	__wh__ istle

Review of Digraphs: Initial and Final /ch/*ch*, /sh/*sh*, /th/*th*;
Final /ch/*tch*. Initial /shr/*shr*, /thr/*thr*, /hw/*wh*

Phonics Practice Book

Name _____

Follow the directions.

1. Circle the chick that is beginning to hatch.
    chick coming out of egg should be circled

2. Draw a watch on the farmer's arm.
    watch should be drawn on the farmer's wrist

3. Draw a ribbon around the white sheep's neck.
    white sheep should have a ribbon around its neck

4. Draw three apples on the branch of the tree.
    there should be three apples on the branch of the tree

5. Draw a shrub by the side of the door.
    shrub should be drawn by one side of the door

6. Circle the sack that has too much grain.
    sack with grain spilling out should be circled

7. Write Cheep! Cheep! over the chicks.
    Cheep! Cheep! should be written over the chicks

8. Draw a thundercloud up in the sky.
    large, dark cloud should be in the sky

9. Circle the rooster on the roof of the barn.
    rooster on the barn should be circled

10. Mark an X on the brush in the farmer's hand.
    brush in the farmer's hand should be marked with an X

11. Draw footprints on the path that leads to the barn door.
    footprints should be drawn on the path

12. Draw a wreath over the horse's door.
    wreath should be on the wall over the horse's door

Phonics Practice Book

Cumulative Review of Digraphs: Initial and Final /ch/*ch*,
Final /ch/*tch*, /sh/*sh*, /th/*th*; Initial /shr/*shr*, /thr/*thr*, /hw/*wh*

229

phone

graph

Choose the word that answers each riddle.
Write the word on the line.

1. I start out in a camera. I end up in an album. I am a
   photo
   _____ .

   photo   pay   phrase

2. I am a chart that shows numbers. I may have lines or bars. I am a
   graph
   _____ .

   graph   great   grill

3. I am more than a word. I am less than a sentence. I am a
   phrase
   _____ .

   phrase   phone   prize

4. I am a name written down. If you meet a sports star, you might
   autograph
   ask for one. I am an _____ .

   enough   autograph   around

5. I am a large bird. I have a long, pretty tail. I am a
   pheasant
   _____ .

   peanut   pheasant   photo

6. I am something you talk into. I am a _____ .
   phone

   phone   picnic   pink

7. I am a group of sentences. I am a _____ .
   paragraph

   graph   paragraph   pillow

8. I am a store where people can buy medicine. I am a
   pharmacy
   _____ .

   pharmacy   farm   phone

laugh

Listen to the sound the letters *gh* stand for in *laugh*. Fill in the circle next to the sentence that tells about the picture.

1		○ We have enough to eat. ○ I like to look at photographs. ○ We will eat indoors.
2		○ The ground feels rough. ○ The dogs sleep on the mat. ◉ The pup thinks he is tough.
3		○ It is fun to read in bed. ◉ Jeff has a cold and a cough. ○ Jeff likes to laugh.
4		○ The bird is in the tree. ◉ The monkey makes us laugh. ○ I took a photo of the tiger.
5		○ I like to swim in the sea. ○ Fran calls me on the phone. ◉ The rough waves rock the boat.
6		○ The pig eats under the tree. ○ The farmer is on the phone. ◉ The horse drinks from the trough.

Name _____

write

Listen to the sound the letters *wr* stand for in *write*. Circle the word that names the picture. Then write the word.

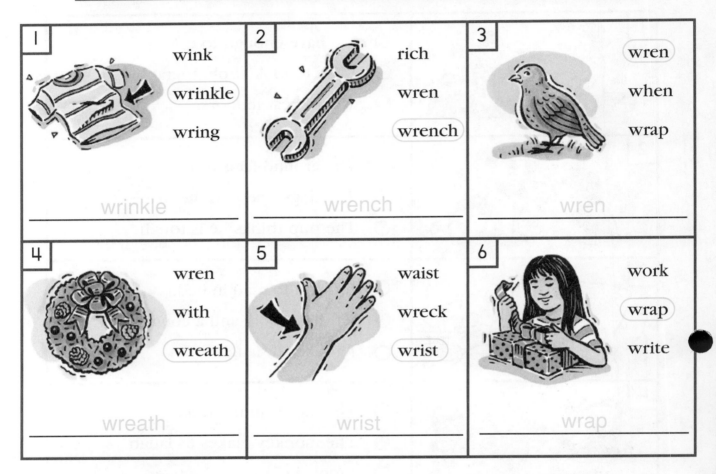

1

wink

(wrinkle)

wring

_____ wrinkle _____

2

rich

wren

(wrench)

_____ wrench _____

3

(wren)

when

wrap

_____ wren _____

4

wren

with

(wreath)

_____ wreath _____

5

waist

wreck

(wrist)

_____ wrist _____

6

work

(wrap)

write

_____ wrap _____

Choose the correct word that answers each clue. Write the word on the line.

7. It means "not right." ___ wrong ___

        rang wing wrong

8. You do this with a pencil or pen. ___ write ___

        write wait read

9. You will find it around a stick of gum or a candy bar. ___ wrapper ___

        rider wrapper wiper

Digraph: Initial /r/wr

Phonics Practice Book

knight

gnat

Listen to the sound the letters *kn* and *gn* stand for in knight and gnat. Complete each sentence.

1. I heard a loud ____knock____ on the door.

cook
knock
night

2. The ____knob____ turned slowly.

not
cob
knob

3. A little green ____gnome____ stood in the doorway.

gnome
gum
name

4. He only came up to my ____knee____.

new
key
knee

5. "Please give me a bone to ____gnaw____ on," he said.

grow
gnaw
gown

6. "I ____know____ you can find one for me," he said.

know
cow
nail

7. "If you do, I will ____knit____ you a cap."

knit
kit
nice

8. As he rode away on a giant ____gnat____, I woke up.

go
gnat
knot

9. Then I ____knew____ it was only a dream.

not
kit
knew

10. But how did this little cap get in my ____knapsack____?

knapsack
napkin
kickoff

Harcourt Brace School Publishers

Name _____

skunk   Listen to the sounds the letters *ng* and *nk* stand for in *ring* and *skunk*.

ring   Read the story and answer the questions.

Eek! A Skunk!

"What are these footprints by the tree trunk?" asked Hank. "Do they belong to a chipmunk?"

"Oh, no!" said Mai Ling. "I hope I am wrong, but I think they belong to a skunk. Look! The prints lead under the porch."

"Here is a hole in the plank," said Hank. "That is its door. We can fix the hole. That will get rid of the skunk."

"Think, Hank!" groaned Mai Ling. "We might fix the hole with the skunk inside. Then the skunk will be angry. It will use its strong smell."

"I know how we can tell," said Hank. "Bring me some flour. We will sprinkle it around the porch. The skunk will walk in the flour. The prints will show where it goes. When the skunk goes out, we can fix the hole."

"Good idea!" said Mai Ling. "Let's do it right now."

Possible responses are shown.

1. Why did Hank and Mai Ling think that the skunk was bad news?

   The skunk might use its strong smell.

2. What can make a skunk use its strong smell?

   making it angry

3. What did Hank want to use to track the skunk?

   flour

Digraphs: Final /ng/*ng*, Final /ngk/*nk* • Reading Words in Context

Phonics Practice Book

Harcourt Brace School Publishers

The words below are hidden in the puzzle. Some words go across. Some words go down. Find and circle each one.

bank   bunk   rink   skunk   king
spring   wing   string   sink   trunk

S	T	R	I	N	G	B	B
I	R	I	N	K	W	U	A
N	U	K	Z	Y	I	N	N
K	N	S	K	U	N	K	K
U	K	K	I	N	G	G	Z
G	X	S	P	R	I	N	G

Write the word from the puzzle that names each picture.

1	2	3	4	5
trunk	king	string	skunk	spring

6	7	8	9	10
wing	bunk	bank	sink	rink

Name _____

REVIEW

Circle the word that names the picture. Then write the word.

1

rough

bath

(laugh)

laugh
_____

2

(wrench)

ring

wren

wrench
_____

3

knit

need

(knee)

knee
_____

4

(gnat)

nap

gnaw

gnat
_____

5

sing

(sink)

sun

sink
_____

6

gray

gift

(graph)

graph
_____

7

with

(wreath)

read

wreath
_____

8

spin

spark

(spring)

spring
_____

9

(phone)

fun

fine

phone
_____

10

stung

shack

(skunk)

skunk
_____

11

(gnome)

note

game

gnome
_____

12

kick

(king)

cane

king
_____

13

(photo)

foot

pot

photo
_____

14

nice

kite

(knight)

knight
_____

15

rink

(ring)

rich

ring
_____

Review of Digraphs: /f/*ph, gh;* /r/*wr;* /n/*kn, gn;*
Final /ng/*ng,* /ngk/*nk*

Phonics Practice Book

Harcourt Brace School Publishers

Name _____

1. Write your name on the sign over the door.
   student's name written on the sign over the door

2. Circle the words that begin with the same sound as *rink*.
   repair and *wrecks* circled

3. Write "THANK YOU" on the sign on the doorknob.
   Thank You written on sign on door knob

4. Draw a bow on the wreath.
   bow drawn on wreath

5. Draw a patch on the knee of the worker's pants.
   patch drawn on knee of pants

6. Circle the wrench.
   the wrench circled

7. Draw an arrow that points to the worker's right wrist.
   arrow drawn pointing to worker's right wrist

8. Write *Ring!* next to the phone.
   word *Ring!* written by the phone

9. Add something to the picture that makes you laugh.
   Responses will vary.

CHECK-UP

Fill in the circle next to the word that names the picture.

1
- ○ chair
- ○ store
- ● shark

shark

2
- ● watch
- ○ what
- ○ rich

watch

3
- ○ gruff
- ● graph
- ○ gray

graph

4
- ○ sink
- ● skunk
- ○ stuck

skunk

5
- ○ bank
- ● branch
- ○ brace

branch

6
- ○ scrub
- ○ skip
- ● shrub

shrub

7
- ○ desk
- ○ dust
- ● dish

dish

8
- ● laugh
- ○ tough
- ○ lift

laugh

9
- ○ wings
- ● swing
- ○ snug

swing

10
- ○ fin
- ● phone
- ○ fan

phone

11
- ● thread
- ○ think
- ○ talk

thread

12
- ○ cup
- ○ champ
- ● chick

chick

13
- ● wren
- ○ rip
- ○ when

wren

14
- ● gnome
- ○ grew
- ○ know

gnome

15
- ○ keep
- ○ need
- ● knee

knee

Digraphs Test

Phonics Practice Book

Name _____

Read the story and find out what happens when Sharman meets a whale.

A WHALE OF A WISH

Sharman loved to watch the sea. One day she saw something big floating near the shore. Sharman could not believe her eyes. It was a whale!

"What are you doing here?" Sharman asked. "Do you know that you are in very shallow water?"

"I am lost," groaned the whale. "If you help me get back to the deep sea, I will grant you a wish."

"Just swing around and follow the sun," said Sharman. "You will be in the deep sea very soon."

"Thank you," said the whale. "Now what is your wish?"

"I'll just wish you home safely," said Sharman. So, with a swish of its tail, the whale swam out to sea.

Fill in the circle next to the correct answer.

1. What did Sharman see floating near the shore?
   ○ some shells
   ◉ a whale
   ○ some cheers

2. What was the whale's problem?
   ◉ The water was too shallow.
   ○ He was near a shark.
   ○ He was sinking.

3. How did Sharman help the whale?
   ○ She swished his tail.
   ○ She gave him a wish.
   ◉ She told him how to find the deep sea.

A shorter way to write *he is* is *he's*. *He's* is a contraction.
To make a contraction, use an apostrophe (') in place of one or
more letters that are left out. In contractions, *am, not, will,* and
is can be shortened to *'m, n't, 'll,* and *'s*.

I am = I'm   can not = can't   she will = she'll

Combine the word at the top of each box with the words below
it to write contractions. Be sure to use an (') to show letters that
are left out.

not		will	
1. could	couldn't	6. he	he'll
2. does	doesn't	7. she	she'll
3. can	can't	8. I	I'll
4. were	weren't	9. you	you'll
5. do	don't		

am

10. I ___ I'm

is

11. he ___ he's   12. she ___ she's   13. it ___ it's

In contractions, *had* and *would* can be shortened to *'d*.
Have and *are* can be shortened to *'ve* and *'re*.

we had = we'd   you have = you've
you would = you'd   they are = they're

Write the two words that make each contraction. Then write the letters that were left out.

Contraction	two words	letters left out
1. I've	I have	ha
2. he'd	he would OR he had	woul OR ha
3. we're	we are	a
4. she'd	she would OR she had	woul OR ha

Write the contraction that can be made by combining the two underlined words. Remember to use an apostrophe (') to show letters that are left out.

5. "You would make a great shortstop," my coach said. _____ You'd _____

6. "I have been thinking about trying that," I said. _____ I've _____

7. "They have got a good shortstop on the other team," said Coach.

_____ They've _____

8. "So, we had better let you practice," he said. _____ we'd _____

Name _____

For each sentence, form a contraction from the words in parentheses ( ). Write the contraction.

New School Rules

1. (I am) (we will) _____I'm_____ about to tell you a couple of new

   rules that _____we'll_____ all need to follow at school.

2. (should not) You _____shouldn't_____ fly an airplane through the door.

3. (cannot) At lunch, your snake _____can't_____ ask for more.

4. (we are) (it is) When _____we're_____ on a field trip,

   _____it's_____ nice to wear your best.

5. (would not) Of course you _____wouldn't_____ come in a wedding

   dress.

6. (You have) _____You've_____ turned in your homework every day,

   I think.

7. (you would) (were not) But _____you'd_____ get a much better

   grade if it _____weren't_____ in invisible ink!

8. (do not) (it will) If you _____don't_____ forget these simple rules,

   _____it'll_____ make for a much happier school.

Harcourt Brace School Publishers

Read the selection. Then answer the questions.

Do you think you'd be surprised at what a magnet can pick up? If you've tried it, you'll know that magnets won't pick up anything that isn't made of a certain material. Do you know what that material is? If you don't, you're about to find out!

A magnet doesn't pick up a piece of paper. It's not going to pick up a pencil, either. What are these two things made from? They're made from wood, of course. What about plastic toys—will a magnet pick them up? No, it won't. What about rocks or glass? A magnet can't move them at all. Could a magnet pick up a metal paper clip? If it couldn't, then it isn't a magnet! Magnets pick up only things that have iron in them. You'll have to test this for yourself some time.

Possible responses are shown.

1. Write a title for the selection that uses a contraction.

What a Magnet Can't Do

_____

2. What are some things that a magnet can't pick up?

rock, glass, plastic, paper, pencil

_____

Name _____

An apostrophe and *s* (*'s*) at the end of a word can show that one person or animal owns something. Read each phrase. If it contains a word that shows someone owns something, write the word. The first one has been done for you.

Chad's bike

1. Ahmed's toy _____Ahmed's_____

2. Grandma's bag _____Grandma's_____

3. flowers growing _____

4. rows of boxes _____

5. cats sleep _____

6. Elena's shorts _____Elena's_____

Change the underlined words in each phrase to one word with *'s*.

7. the desk <u>that belongs to my brother</u>

   my _____brother's_____ desk

8. the necklace <u>that belongs to Mom</u>

   _____Mom's_____ necklace

9. the hat <u>that belongs to the firefighter</u>

   the _____firefighter's_____ hat

10. The skates <u>that belong to Connie</u>

    _____Connie's_____ skates

244   Possessive: *'s*

Harcourt Brace School Publishers

Phonics Practice Book

An *s* and an apostrophe (*s'*) at the end of a word can show that more than one person or animal owns something.

Read the first sentence in each pair. In the second sentence, write the underlined word in a way that shows that more than one person or animal owns or has something.

my parent<u>s'</u> car

1. We saw several <u>puppies</u> at the shelter.

   The _____puppies'_____ coats had black spots.

2. Ken picked up the toys belonging to the <u>kittens</u>.

   Now the _____kittens'_____ toys are put away.

3. The bikes that belong to the <u>girls</u> are in the driveway.

   We need to move the _____girls'_____ bikes.

4. Our <u>friends</u> ordered a cheese pizza.

   We will share our _____friends'_____ pizza.

5. The crops of the <u>farmers</u> are good this year.

   The fruit stand is full of the _____farmers'_____ crops.

6. The <u>boys</u> were out on the beach too long.

   Now the _____boys'_____ faces are red.

7. Boxes of new books came in for the <u>teachers</u>.

   The _____teachers'_____ books are in the classroom.

8. Mr. Moon took photos of all of the <u>classes</u>.

   The _____classes'_____ photos turned out well.

REVIEW

Read the book titles. Write words from the titles in the correct places on the chart.

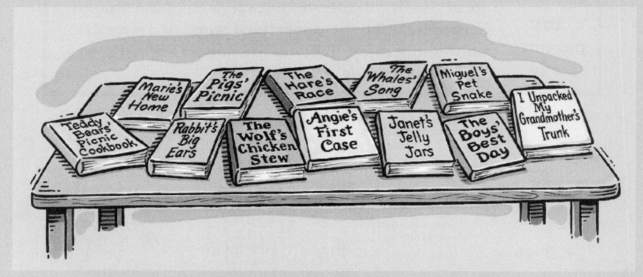

Words That Show One Owner	Words That Show More Than One Owner
Marie's	Bears'
Rabbit's	Pigs'
Wolf's	Whales'
Hare's	Boys'
Angie's	
Janet's	
Miguel's	
Grandmother's	

Review of Possessives

Phonics Practice Book

Name _____

Look at the number of animals in each picture. Label each home to show whether it belongs to one animal or more than one animal.

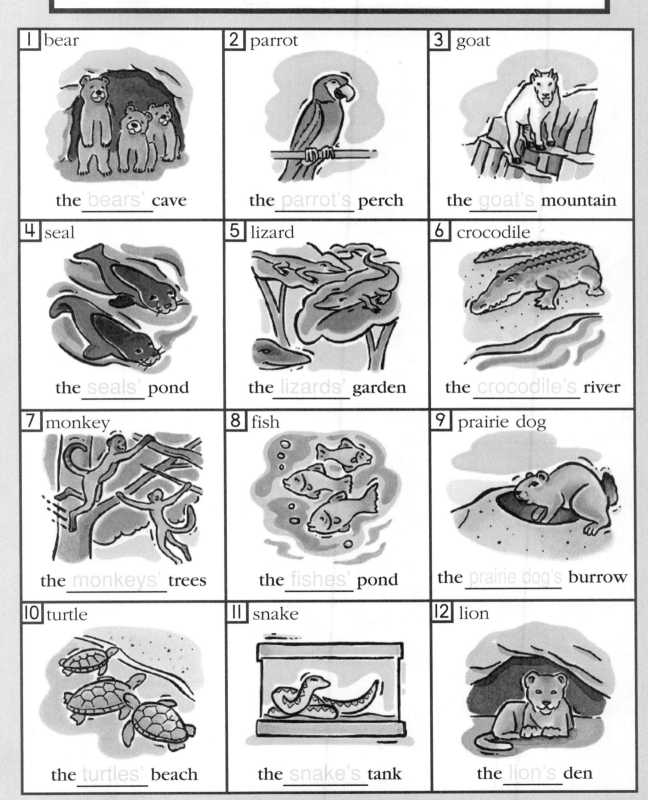

1 | bear
the bears' cave

2 | parrot
the parrot's perch

3 | goat
the goat's mountain

4 | seal
the seals' pond

5 | lizard
the lizards' garden

6 | crocodile
the crocodile's river

7 | monkey
the monkeys' trees

8 | fish
the fishes' pond

9 | prairie dog
the prairie dog's burrow

10 | turtle
the turtles' beach

11 | snake
the snake's tank

12 | lion
the lion's den

Write the two words that each contraction stands for.

1. shouldn't   should _____   not _____

2. haven't   have _____   not _____

3. it's   it _____   is _____

4. you'd   you _____   would OR had _____

5. they're   they _____   are _____

6. I'm   I _____   am _____

7. we'll   we _____   will _____

8. you're   you _____   are _____

9. I've   I _____   have _____

10. he'd   he _____   would OR had _____

11. she's   she _____   is _____

12. they'll   they _____   will _____

13. couldn't   could _____   not _____

14. they'd   they _____   would OR had _____

Harcourt Brace School Publishers

Change the underlined words in each phrase to a word with 's or s'.

CHECK-UP

1. the watch <u>that belongs to Ann</u>   ____Ann's____ watch

2. the shirt <u>that belongs to Adam</u>   ____Adam's____ shirt

3. the bikes <u>that belong to the boys</u>   the ____boys'____ bikes

4. the houses <u>that belong to the dogs</u>   the ____dogs'____ houses

5. the letter <u>that belongs to Amy</u>   ____Amy's____ letter

6. the suitcase <u>that belongs to our friends</u>   our ____friends'____ suitcase

7. the song <u>that Grandpa wrote</u>   ____Grandpa's____ song

8. the shadow <u>made by Rico</u>   ____Rico's____ shadow

9. the hot dog <u>that belongs to Mrs. French</u>   ____Mrs. French's____ hot dog

10. the feathers <u>that the ducks have</u>   the ____ducks'____ feathers

11. the sounds <u>of the horns</u>   the ____horns'____ sounds

12. the screens <u>that go with the computers</u>   the ____computers'____ screens

13. the keys <u>that belong to the teacher</u>   the ____teacher's____ keys

14. the wings <u>that the butterflies have</u>   the ____butterflies'____ wings

15. the cake <u>for the twins</u>   the ____twins'____ cake

Complete each sentence by adding *s*, *es*, *ed*, or *ing* to the word in front of the sentence.

Today
I jump.
The frog jump<u>s</u> too.
The frog and I are jump<u>ing</u>.
My dad watch<u>es</u> us.
Yesterday
The frog jump<u>ed</u>, and I did not.

1. play   The Lan family enjoys _____*playing*_____ music every day.

2. start   The children _____*started*_____ playing when they
         were very young.

3. sing   Mei Ling _____*sings*_____ and plays the flute.

4. want   Tran plays the violin, but last year he _____*wanted*_____
         to learn to play the harp.

5. wish   He _____*wishes or wished*_____ he could play both.

6. listen Mrs. Lan smiles as she _____*listens*_____ to her
         children play.

7. talk   Last week, they _____*talked*_____ about
         giving a concert.

8. look   They are _____*looking*_____ for
         a place to hold a concert.

9. ask   Last Tuesday, the Lans _____*asked*_____ me to help them find
         a place.

10. wait   The Lans are just _____*waiting*_____ for the special day when
         they can give the concert.

Inflected Endings: -s, -es, -ed, -ing   Phonics Practice Book

Harcourt Brace School Publishers

Name _____

	Base Word	Base Word + *s* or *es*	Base Word + *ed*	Base Word + *ing*
1	discuss	discusses	discussed	discussing
2	thank	thanks	thanked	thanking
3	talk	talks	talked	talking
4	work	works	worked	working
5	clean	cleans	cleaned	cleaning

Use a word from the chart to complete each sentence.

6. Last month we _____discussed_____ our trip to visit a city worker.

7. Today we arrived at the park, and the city worker _____talked_____ to our class.

8. He _____works_____ hard to keep parks and streams clean.

9. We say we will help, and now we are _____cleaning_____ up a stream.

10. The city worker _____thanks_____ us for helping him.

In most short-vowel words that end with one consonant, double the final consonant before adding *ed* or *ing*.

Today	**Yesterday**
Pam and I jog.	Yesterday, it rained
Sam is jogg<u>ing</u> too.	while Pam jogg<u>ed</u>.

Double the final consonant before adding *ed* and *ing* to each base word. Write the words.

1 clap	2 put	3 grab
clapped	put	grabbed
clapping	putting	grabbing

4 stop	5 plan	6 run
stopped	planned	ran
stopping	planning	running

Use a word from above to complete each sentence. You will not use all of the words.

7. Yesterday we _____ planned _____ to go for a swim when my cousin arrived.

8. Today my cousin is here, and we are _____ running _____ to the lake.

9. Now we are _____ putting _____ on our swim fins.

10. When we get out of the water, we will _____ grab _____ our towels.

Inflected Endings: *-ed, -ing*

Harcourt Brace School Publishers

Add *ed* to the first group of words to tell what Pat did yesterday. Add *ing* to the next group of words to tell what Pat is doing today.

What Pat Did Yesterday

mop   jog   clap

mopped

jogged

clapped

What Pat Is Doing Today

swim   chat   dig

swimming

chatting

digging

Add *ed* or *ing* to the underlined word to complete the second sentence in each pair.

1. My mom and I <u>plant</u> flowers in the garden.

   We are _____*planting*_____ two different kinds of flowers.

2. Mom and I each <u>dig</u> a hole in the ground.

   I am _____*digging*_____ a deeper hole than Mom's.

3. I <u>put</u> a pretty daisy in the hole.

   Mom is _____*putting*_____ in an orange geranium.

4. I <u>pat</u> the soil around my flower.

   Mom is _____*patting*_____ the soil around her flower more firmly than I am.

5. Now we <u>pour</u> water on our flowers.

   The last time we planted flowers, I _____*poured*_____ too much water on mine.

Read the paragraphs, and think about what they tell you.

An Eclipse of the Sun

Have you ever seen an eclipse of the sun? Bet you were wondering what was happening. If so, you saw the sky get dark in the middle of the day.

People long ago were afraid when there was an eclipse. They would start running and screaming. But we know now that an eclipse is nothing to be afraid of.

An eclipse happens when the moon passes in a straight line between the earth and the sun. For a short time, the moon blocks the light of the sun. Then the moon passes out of the way, and sunlight once again touches the earth.

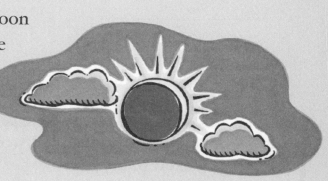

Write the answers to the questions.

1. What happens to the sky during an eclipse of the sun?

   It gets dark.

2. What brings about an eclipse of the sun?

   The moon passes between the sun and the earth.

3. How does an eclipse of the sun end?

   The moon passes out of the way of the sun's light.

4. Long ago, what did people do when they saw an eclipse?

   They screamed and ran. They were afraid.

Review of Inflected Endings: -s, -es, -ed, -ing

Harcourt Brace School Publishers

Add the correct ending to the underlined base word in each sentence. Write the new words in the puzzle.

Across

1. My canary <u>sing</u> as I eat my breakfast.
3. The girl is <u>bring</u> some food for her pet.
5. My cat <u>rub</u> against my legs last night.
7. The rabbit <u>munch</u> on the carrots I give it.
9. My cat <u>purr</u> when I stroked her fur yesterday.
11. The boy <u>hunt</u> for his lost book last week.
13. I am <u>run</u> in a race today.

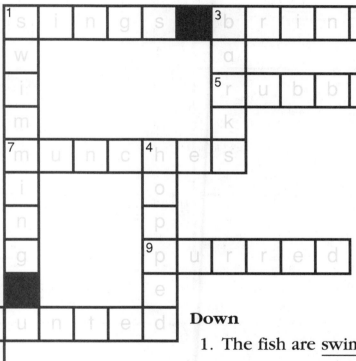

Down

1. The fish are <u>swim</u> in the tank.
2. We are <u>pat</u> soil around the new plants.
3. The dog <u>bark</u> as a stranger passes by.
4. The frog <u>hop</u> onto the lily pad just a minute ago.
11. That girl is <u>hum</u> while she walks to school.

In words that end with silent *e*, drop the *e* before adding *ed* or *ing*. Drop the silent *e* and add *ed* and *ing* to each base word. Write the new words.

Dad and I bake cakes and pies.

Dad bak<u>ed</u> a cake yesterday.

Dad is bak<u>ing</u> a pie today.

1 save	2 slice
saved	sliced
saving	slicing

3 rake	4 tape
raked	taped
raking	taping

5 name	6 dance
named	danced
naming	dancing

7 race	8 paste
raced	pasted
racing	pasting

Name _____

Today I am writing about my trip to my grandma's house. Last Saturday, my friend Trina and I went to my grandma's house in the country. Grandma brought us a picnic lunch and we walked down to the stream.

After we ate, we waded in the water. For a while, we bounced rocks across the stream. Trina got bored, so we raced back to the house. Grandma had a surprise. She had just baked a peach pie! She gave us some with ice cream.

When it was time to leave, Trina told Grandma and me she had had a great day. She said she could not remember ever having so much fun. I loved it, too. I always enjoy going to Grandma's house.

Possible responses are shown.

1. Name three things the girls did at Grandma's house.

   They walked down to a stream, ate a picnic lunch, and waded

   in the stream

2. How does the girl feel about going to her grandma's house? How do you know?

   She loves it. She says she always enjoys going to her house.

3. What was Grandma's surprise?

   She had baked a peach pie.

In a word that ends in *f* or *fe*, change the *f* or *fe* to *v* and add *es* to make it mean more than one. Add *es* to each word. Write the new word.

one wol**f**

two wol**ves**

one kni**fe**

two kni**ves**

1	knife	2	elf
	knives		elves
3	leaf	**4**	thief
	leaves		thieves
5	life	**6**	loaf
	lives		loaves
7	shelf	**8**	half
	shelves		halves
9	wife	**10**	calf
	wives		calves

Use a word from above to complete each sentence.

11. Mom baked three _____loaves_____ of bread today.

12. We ate apple _____halves_____ for a snack at school.

13. Mr. Brown let us feed the _____calves_____ on his farm.

14. Sam and Pete raked the _____leaves_____ in Mrs. Smith's yard.

Inflected Ending: *-es*

Phonics Practice Book

Harcourt Brace School Publishers

In a base word that ends with a consonant followed by *y*, drop the *y* before adding *ies*. For each base word below, drop the final *y* and add *ies*. Write the new word.

The baby can cr_y_. The baby cries.

1 spy	2 copy	3 fly
spies	copies	flies
_____	_____	_____

4 carry	5 try	6 hurry
carries	tries	hurries
_____	_____	_____

Use a word from above to complete each sentence.

7. A cat _____ spies _____ a butterfly resting on a flower.

8. The cat _____ tries _____ to chase the butterfly.

9. The butterfly _____ flies _____ away quickly.

10. The cat _____ hurries _____ after it, but still it cannot

catch the beautiful butterfly.

Read the story and answer the questions.

My aunt works in a diner. She likes her job. I like to go to see her there. The food is good, and the people are friendly. The diner is busy.

My aunt takes people's orders and carries out the food on a big tray. She rushes around and hurries to get people the things they ask for. She says she always tries to be friendly and nice to people.

After the diner is closed, my aunt dries the dishes. Sometimes I help, too. When we get home, she empties her pockets, and I count her tips. She studies the newspaper. Sometimes she spies on me to make sure I am counting the money right!

Possible responses are shown.

1. Why does the boy like the diner?

His aunt works there, it has good food, and the people are friendly.

2. Name four things the boy's aunt does at her job in the diner.

She takes people's orders; she carries out the food; she gets

people things they ask for; she dries the dishes.

3. What would be a good title for this story?

At Work with My Aunt

Inflected Ending: *-ies* • Reading Words in Context

Phonics Practice Book

Harcourt Brace School Publishers

Name _____

Read the book titles. Then write the base word for each word in the boxes.

SUPER REVIEW

Write the base word for each of these words from the titles.

1 grows grow	2 smiling smile
3 cries cry	4 scarves scarf
5 stopped stop	6 loved love
7 giving give	8 sleeps sleep
9 bringing bring	10 scared scare

Harcourt Brace School Publishers

Write the base word for the underlined word in each sentence.

1. Our dad <u>tries</u> to teach us to do things to help clean up the earth. _____ try _____

2. He <u>likes</u> for us to recycle paper and cans each week. _____ like _____

3. He also <u>wants</u> us to grow some of our own food. _____ want _____

4. My little sister and I <u>planted</u> some bean seeds in pots. _____ plant _____

5. Dad said, "Put them in the window and make sure the sun is <u>shining</u> on them."
_____ shine _____

6. Every day my sister <u>rushes</u> over to look at the pots. _____ rush _____

7. Earlier this morning she shouted, "They <u>sprouted</u> last night!" _____ sprout _____

8. My little sister <u>clapped</u> her hands when she saw the tiny plants. _____ clap _____

9. I saw little green shoots <u>popping</u> up through the soil. _____ pop _____

10. Soon we will be <u>eating</u> the beans that we have grown. _____ eat _____

11. My dad has <u>asked</u> us to think of some other ways we can keep the earth
clean. _____ ask _____

12. He says our <u>lives</u> will be better if the earth is clean and healthy.
_____ life _____

Write the base word for the underlined word in each sentence.

1. Last week we <u>planned</u> a camping trip. _____plan_____

2. Today we are <u>staying</u> in a tent at our beautiful campsite. _____stay_____

3. The sun is <u>shining</u> brightly. _____shine_____

4. But every time we leave the campsite, a bear <u>tries</u> to get our food. _____try_____

5. Mom <u>fusses</u> at us if we leave food sitting out. _____fuss_____

6. We are <u>hoping</u> the bear has gotten tired of our campsite, but it hasn't. _____hope_____

7. It keeps <u>walking</u> up to our campsite when we are not there. _____walk_____

8. A little while ago, we tried to go back to the tent but we <u>stopped</u> when we saw the bear. _____stop_____

9. It was eating all of our <u>loaves</u> of honey bread. _____loaf_____

10. Dad <u>wants</u> to scare the bear away. _____want_____

11. We are <u>getting</u> tired of waiting. _____get_____

12. Finally the bear <u>runs</u> away! _____run_____

Name _____

Complete the chart by adding the ending at the top to the base word.

		s or es	ing	ed
1	start	starts	starting	started
2	skid	skids	skidding	skidded
3	wish	wishes	wishing	wished
4	play	plays	playing	played
5	watch	watches	watching	watched
6	clap	claps	clapping	clapped

Write the base word.

7	grabbed _grab_	8	sings _sing_	9	trying _try_
10	dishes _dish_	11	leaves _leaf_	12	stopping _stop_
13	spies _spy_	14	picked _pick_	15	chatting _chat_
16	pitches _pitch_	17	dries _dry_	18	taped _tape_

A prefix is added to the beginning of a base word to make a new word with a different meaning. Write the word with *un-* or *re-* that matches each meaning.

un = not
re = again

1	use again	2	not kind	3	join again
	reuse		unkind		rejoin

4	build again	5	not able	6	write again
	rebuild		unable		rewrite

7	not true	8	not happy	9	fill again
	untrue		unhappy		refill

10	not afraid	11	tell again	12	not safe
	unafraid		retell		unsafe

Add the prefix *im-* to each word. Then write a word to complete each sentence.

im = not

13	patient	14	perfect	15	polite
	impatient		imperfect		impolite

16. My family says that being late is

_____ impolite _____

17. When we are getting ready to go somewhere,

they are quite _____ impatient _____ with me.

18. I think that makes them _____ imperfect _____, too!

Name _____

Add the prefix *im-* or *re-* to the underlined word to complete each sentence.

1. If water is not clean and <u>pure</u>, then it is _____impure_____.

2. If you <u>check</u> your work again, you _____recheck_____ it.

3. If you <u>pay</u> back money that you owe, you _____repay_____ it.

4. If you <u>tie</u> your shoe again, you _____retie_____ it.

5. If an action is not <u>proper</u>, then it is _____improper_____.

6. If someone is not <u>mature</u>, then he or she is _____immature_____.

7. If you <u>place</u> an item back on the shelf, you _____replace_____ it.

8. If something is not <u>possible</u>, then it is _____impossible_____.

9. If you <u>read</u> a book a second time, you _____reread_____ it.

10. If you turn in work that is not <u>perfect</u>, it might be called
    _____imperfect_____.

Add the prefix *re-* to each base word.

11. pack   _____repack_____

12. cover   _____recover_____

13. load   _____reload_____

14. tie   _____retie_____

15. do   _____redo_____

Harcourt Brace School Publishers

Read the selection, and then answer the question.

Bats Bats Bats

Many stories told about bats are untrue. That is why people may react badly when they see bats. Many things that bats do in stories and movies are impossible. Bats can fly like birds. But unlike birds, bats are mammals. All other mammals are unable to fly.

Many bats live in caves. If you go during the day to see bats fly out of a cave, you may become impatient. Bats sleep all day, hanging upside down. At sunset they unfold their wings. Then they fly out of the cave to rejoin the outside world.

Bats fly around looking for food. They help people by eating insects that are pests. So, the next time you see a bat, don't be afraid. If someone tells you something unlikely about bats, ask the person to recheck his or her facts.

Possible responses are shown.

1. What can be said of many of the things bats do in stories and movies?

   They are impossible.

2. Why do some people react badly when they see bats?

   They have heard many untrue stories about bats.

3. How does the selection say bats are different from birds?

   Bats are mammals.

4. How do bats spend their time during the day?

   They sleep all day.

5. How do bats help people?

   They eat insects that are pests.

Prefixes: *un-, re-, im-*

Harcourt Brace School Publishers

non = not or without   **pre** = before   **dis** = the opposite of
Use the prefixes *non, pre,* and *dis* to write a word to match each meaning.

1 not a believer	2 to pay before	3 the opposite of *like*
nonbeliever	prepay	dislike
4 not making sense	5 to judge before the right time	6 the opposite of *honest*
nonsense	prejudge	dishonest
7 not toxic	8 to plan before	9 to view before
nontoxic	preplan	preview
10 without a stop	11 the opposite of *appear*	12 the opposite of *order*
nonstop	disappear	disorder

Use a word you just wrote to complete each sentence. You will not use all of the words.

13. The messy room was in a state of ___disorder___.

14. Something was sure to get lost and ___disappear___.

15. We sat down to ___preplan___ who would do the job.

16. Then we worked ___nonstop___ to get the work done.

Phonics Practice Book

Name _____

Add the prefix *pre-* or *dis-* to the underlined word to complete each sentence.

1. If you do not <u>continue</u> to play a game, you _____discontinue_____ it.

2. If you are not yet a <u>teen</u>, you are a _____preteen_____.

3. If you do not feel <u>comfort</u>, then you might feel _____discomfort_____.

4. The steps a pilot follows before a <u>flight</u> are called _____preflight_____ checks.

5. Things that happened before <u>historic</u> times are _____prehistoric_____.

6. A baseball team that does not have the <u>advantage</u> of having good hitters is usually at a _____disadvantage_____.

Add the prefix *non-* to each base word.

7. verbal

_____nonverbal_____

8. skid

_____nonskid_____

9. sense

_____nonsense_____

10. stop

_____nonstop_____

Write a word you just wrote to complete each sentence.

11. Mom says that buying fancy tennis shoes is _____nonsense_____.

12. I think good shoes are important when you play sports _____nonstop_____.

13. I even told her that the _____nonskid_____ soles would keep me from slipping.

14. She did not say anything, but her _____nonverbal_____ clues still told me "no."

Read the selection, and answer the questions.

What Happened to the Dinosaurs?

Experts disagree about what happened to the creatures that predated other animals. Some scientists say that the dinosaurs disappeared because of changes in the weather. They think it became too cold for dinosaurs to live.

Other scientists say that a huge meteor crashed into the Earth. They think clouds of dust killed many kinds of plants. Many dinosaurs would have had nothing to eat.

Since there are no records of that time, it is hard to disprove one idea or the other. People may wonder for a long time what really happened to those prehistoric creatures. Until proof is found, people can study dinosaurs' nonextinct relatives—reptiles and birds.

Possible responses are shown.

1. Why could a meteor have caused dinosaurs to die out?

   The dust would have destroyed plants, leaving many dinosaurs

   with nothing to eat.

2. Why is it hard to disprove ideas about dinosaurs?

   There are no records of that time.

3. What nonextinct relatives of dinosaurs can we study today?

   reptiles and birds

Prefixes: *non-, pre-, dis-* • Reading Words in Context

Harcourt Brace School Publishers

Name _____

The words below are in the puzzle. Some words go down. Some words go across. Find and circle each one.

prejudge	disband	improper	undo	nonstick	pretest
untrue	refill	nonsense	disobey	impolite	reheat

```
i   m   p   r   o   p   e   r   b
b   d   i   s   b   a   n   d   l
z   t   v   j   i   q   a   d   m
q   j   p   r   e   t   e   s   t
i   k   n   n   j   b   k   e   n
e   p   r   x   v   q   b   k   o
l   r   e   h   e   a   t   c   n
u   e   g   u   n   d   o   b   s
t   j   h   c   b   w   m   o   t
t   u   n   t   r   u   e   k   i
i   d   i   s   o   b   e   y   c
g   g   o   p   r   i   x   t   k
r   e   f   i   l   l   n   z   u
n   o   n   s   e   n   s   e   p
r   i   m   p   o   l   i   t   e
```

Write a word you circled in the puzzle to answer each question.

1. This word means "to not obey."   _disobey_

2. This word means "to fill again."   _refill_

3. This word means "to judge before."   _prejudge_

4. This word means "not true."   _untrue_

REVIEW

Read the letter, and answer the questions.

Dear Misha,

　　Did you know that some kinds of wolves are in danger of becoming extinct? Some people in my state are trying to rebuild the wolf population in my area. It is uncertain whether they will be able to help. Some people dislike the idea of having wolves rejoin the wildlife here. They feel it will be unsafe for farm animals. But I think that's nonsense. If the wolves don't get help, it will be impossible for them to recover and live in the wild. What do you think? I'd like to hear whether you agree or disagree with me.

　　Your pen pal,
　　Josh

Possible responses are shown.

1. Why did Josh write to Misha?

　　_____to tell him about wolves in danger_____

2. Why is Josh not sure if the group will be able to help the wolves?

　　_____Some people are upset by the group's efforts._____

3. Why do some people dislike the idea of the wolves rejoining the local

　　wildlife? _____They think wolves will harm farm animals._____

4. What does Josh think about wolves?

　　_____He likes them. He wants to help them._____

Harcourt Brace School Publishers

Name _____

The suffixes *-ly* and *-ful* can be added to the end of base words to change their meaning.

      -ly = in a certain way   -ful = full of or enough to fill

Add the suffix to each word below it. Write the new words.

-ly

1. slow _____ slowly _____
2. loud _____ loudly _____
3. quiet _____ quietly _____
4. neat _____ neatly _____
5. quick _____ quickly _____
6. poor _____ poorly _____

-ful

7. care _____ careful _____
8. help _____ helpful _____
9. thought _____ thoughtful _____
10. thank _____ thankful _____
11. cheer _____ cheerful _____
12. hope _____ hopeful _____

Use some of the new words you made to complete the sentences.

13. I wanted to finish my homework _____ quickly _____ so I could go outside and play.

14. I wrote my spelling words _____ neatly _____ so that they were easy to read.

15. I had a question about my math homework, and my sister was _____ helpful _____.

16. I was _____ thankful _____ that she could help.

17. I closed my books and _____ quietly _____ put my things away.

18. My sister said that I was _____ thoughtful _____ for being so quiet.

Suffixes: *-ly, -ful*

Name _____

Add -ly or -ful to each base word to complete each sentence.

---

1. care   We are always _____careful_____ when we cross the street.

2. safe   The crossing guard helps us get _____safely_____ to the other side.

3. brave   She _____bravely_____ stops traffic for us.

4. near   One day there was _____nearly_____ an accident.

5. foolish A little boy _____foolishly_____ dashed in front of a car.

6. Fortunate _____Fortunately_____ ,the car was able to stop.

7. quick   If the driver had not reacted _____quickly_____ , the boy could have been hurt.

8. fear   The driver was _____fearful_____ that someone had been hurt.

9. thank   When she saw that no one was hurt, she looked _____thankful_____ .

10. tear   The little boy was fine but _____tearful_____ .

11. help   The crossing guard was _____helpful_____ in getting the boy to calm down.

12. kind   The guard _____kindly_____ explained to the boy what he should do next time.

Suffixes: -ly, -ful   Phonics Practice Book

able = able to be, able to give   less = without

Add the suffix *-able* or *-less* to write a word to match each definition.

1 able to be washed	2 without joy	3 able to give comfort
washable	joyless	comfortable
_____	_____	_____

4 without sleep	5 able to be noticed	6 able to be remarked upon
sleepless	noticeable	remarkable
_____	_____	_____

7 without a care	8 without thought	9 able to be worked
careless	, thoughtless	workable
_____	_____	_____

Add *-able* or *-less* to the base word to complete each phrase.

10. port _____portable_____ television

11. sugar _____sugarless_____ gum

12. value _____valuable_____ jewelry
    (hint: drop the final *e*)

13. seed _____seedless_____ grapes

14. adore _____adorable_____ teddy bear (hint: drop the final *e*)

15. love _____lovable_____ pet (hint: drop the final *e*)

Name _____

Choose the word that completes each sentence. Write the words in the puzzle.

toothless   thoughtless   cloudless
washable   remarkable   tasteless
adorable   helpless   portable

ACROSS

1. Water has no taste. It is _____.
3. My radio is easy to take with me because it is _____.
5. The sky was clear and _____.
7. The baby had a _____ grin.

DOWN

1. Leaving without saying goodbye was _____.
2. I read the most _____ story.
4. I am glad my new shirt is _____.
6. I try to solve my own problems rather than be _____.
10. The new puppy was _____ .

Suffixes: *-able, -less*

Phonics Practice Book

Add the correct suffix to the underlined word to complete each sentence.

REVIEW

-less   -able
-ly   -ful

1. If the night sky seems to have not even one <u>star</u>, then

    it is ____starless____ .

2. If you are moving at a <u>slow</u> speed, you are moving ____slowly____ .

3. If your jeans can be put in the <u>wash</u>, they are ____washable____ .

4. If you have enough sugar to fill one <u>cup</u>, you have a ____cupful____ .

5. If you enjoy the <u>comfort</u> of your bed, it is a ____comfortable____ place.

6. If you are full of <u>joy</u>, you are ____joyful____ .

7. If you did not <u>sleep</u> last night, you had a ____sleepless____ night.

8. If you speak in a <u>loud</u> way, your family might say you

    speak ____loudly____ .

9. If you had a day full of <u>wonder</u>, you had a ____wonderful____ day.

10. If you are brave and without <u>fear</u>, you are a ____fearless____ person.

11. If you can <u>train</u> your pet to do tricks, your pet is ____trainable____ .

12. If you are finishing this page in a <u>quick</u> way, you are

    finishing ____quickly____ .

REVIEW

Write a word to complete each sentence.

| cupful fearless careful lovely quickly sleepless |
| neatly remarkable moveable kindly mouthful slowly |

1. Please be ___careful___ when you hold the new puppy.

2. That animal trick was amazing and ___remarkable___.

3. Please write your name ___neatly___ on the page.

4. The firefighters were brave and ___fearless___ during the blaze.

5. It is impolite to talk with a ___mouthful___ of food.

6. My neighbor would like to borrow a ___cupful___ of sugar.

7. The police officer spoke ___kindly___ to the lost child.

8. This toy has a lot of ___moveable___ parts.

9. We spent a ___sleepless___ night because the storm was so loud.

10. Mom said the painting I made was ___lovely___.

11. The small rabbit ran away ___quickly___ when it saw the fox.

12. I chew my food ___slowly___ so I can enjoy every bite.

Harcourt Brace School Publishers

Name _____

Write the word from the box that fits each meaning.

impolite   prejudge   lovable   unsafe   washable
sugarless   blameless   neatly   softly   dislike
reread   fearful   nonstop   dishonest   joyful

1. able to be washed ___washable___

2. in a neat way ___neatly___

3. without sugar ___sugarless___

4. to read again ___reread___

5. without a stop ___nonstop___

6. in a soft way ___softly___

7. to judge before the right time ___prejudge___

8. without blame ___blameless___

9. able to be loved ___lovable___

10. full of joy ___joyful___

11. not safe ___unsafe___

12. opposite of honest ___dishonest___

13. not polite ___impolite___

14. full of fear ___fearful___

15. the opposite of *like* ___dislike___

Write the prefix or suffix that completes each statement.

1. ____pre____ + historic = before historic times

2. tender + ____ly____ = in a tender way

3. ____re____ + pack = to pack again

4. ____non____ + sense = not making sense

5. ____dis____ + agree = the opposite of *agree*

6. cup + ____ful____ = amount to fill a cup

7. ____un____ + opened = not opened

8. ____im____ + possible = not possible

9. thought + ____less____ = without thought

10. train + ____able____ = able to be trained

11. ____un____ + certain = not certain

12. sleep + ____less____ = without sleep

13. ____dis____ + obey = the opposite of *obey*

14. ____un____ + healthy = not healthy

Harcourt Brace School Publishers

Name _____

> **Add *-er* and *-est* to each word. Write the new words in the chart.**

Beth is *tall.*	Kim is *taller* than Beth. Word + *-er*	Mary is the *tallest* one. Word + *-est*
1. fresh	fresher	freshest
2. kind	kinder	kindest
3. sweet	sweeter	sweetest
4. light	lighter	lightest
5. hard	harder	hardest
6. warm	warmer	warmest
7. long	longer	longest
8. loud	louder	loudest
9. short	shorter	shortest
10. clear	clearer	clearest

> **Use some of the new words you wrote to complete the sentences.**

11. I like the summer when the days get longer. In fact, the

_____longest_____ day of the year is in June.

12. In June the weather gets _____warmer_____ with each day that passes.

13. I begin to wear shorts and _____lighter_____ clothing to keep cool.

14. The vegetables from our garden taste _____fresher_____ than the ones

from the store.

15. Summer is when we get the _____sweetest_____ peaches, berries, and

melons.

Name _____

Read the first sentence in each pair. Complete the second sentence by adding *er* or *est* to the word in bold print.

1	Allen is **strong.** Jack is _____ stronger _____.
2 	Ann's sweater is **warm.** Her mom's coat is _____ warmer _____.
3 	All of the pencils are **short.** The pencil on the right is the _____ shortest _____.
4 	The penny is **light.** The feather is _____ lighter _____.
5 	The boys on the team are **tall.** The boy at the end of the line is the _____ tallest _____.
6 	The rope is **strong.** The chain is even _____ stronger _____.
7	Michael wore a **dark** cap to the game. His dad wore a _____ darker _____ one.

Comparatives and Superlatives: *-er, -est*   Phonics Practice Book

> **Look at the picture, and follow the directions.**

This is the _____ comfortable chair of all.

1. Write *We Have the Most Affordable Prices in Town* on the wall.
   We Have the Most Affordable Prices in Town is written on the wall

2. Circle the table with a lamp that is more expensive.
   table marked $150 is circled

3. Complete the girl's thought.
   the girl's thought is completed with the word most

4. Draw flowers in the vase to make the room look more beautiful.
   flowers are drawn in the vase

5. Draw two pillows on the most expensive couch.
   two pillows are drawn on the couch marked $500

6. Put an X on the more slender lamp.
   an X is drawn on the more slender lamp

7. Complete these sentences with *more* or *most*.

• The middle couch is _____more_____ expensive than the left one.

• The white couch is the _____most_____ expensive one of all.

Name _____

My sister is intelligent—
Awards hang on her wall.
But even more intelligent
Is my big brother, Paul.

I'm good at math and science.
A whiz at basketball.
It's clear to me that I'm the most
Intelligent of all.

My mom says, "Be more modest,
Like Sis and brother Paul."
I'm modest—clearly, I am the
Most modest one of all!

Possible responses are shown.

1. What does the speaker of the poem think of himself? He is
   the most intelligent and most modest member of his
   family.

2. Write some advice for the boy who is speaking in the poem.
   People should not compare themselves with others;
   people should not brag about themselves.

3. What would be a good title for this poem? _____
   Accept reasonable responses.

Comparatives and Superlatives: *more, most*

Phonics Practice Book

doctor

teacher

The endings *er* and *or* can sometimes show the job a person does. Write the job name below next to its description.

shipper	farmer	painter	pitcher
plumber	seller	doctor	sculptor
actor	teacher	donor	writer

1. a person who fixes plumbing _____plumber_____

2. a person who makes sculptures _____sculptor_____

3. a person who donates something _____donor_____

4. a person who acts _____actor_____

5. a person who ships things _____shipper_____

6. a person who farms _____farmer_____

7. a person who pitches baseballs _____pitcher_____

8. a person who writes _____writer_____

9. a person who cares for other people's health _____doctor_____

10. a person who paints things _____painter_____

11. a person who teaches _____teacher_____

12. a person who sells things _____seller_____

Write the word that best completes each sentence.

> writer actor farmer
> painter sculptor plumber
> doctor officer speaker teacher

It's fun to think about the jobs I could have someday. I like to put things

together. Once I saw a _____plumber_____ putting the pipes and drains in a

new house. I also like to make old things look new. I once saw a

_____painter_____ make an old house look great by putting fresh paint on it.

I like music and the arts, too. I love to put my hands in clay and make

things from it, so I might become a _____sculptor_____. I enjoy thinking up

new stories and writing them on paper. It might be fun to be a

_____writer_____, and have people read my stories. I like to act stories

out, too. I wonder if I could be a movie or television _____actor_____.

Since I am good at growing things, I might become a

_____farmer_____. I like to help other people learn new things, so I might

make a good _____teacher_____. It would be exciting to be a police

_____officer_____ to help people stay safe. Or maybe I will become a

_____doctor_____ and help people stay healthy.

Since I have so many ideas about

jobs, maybe I'll spend more time

speaking with others about their jobs.

That's it—I'll become a famous

_____speaker_____!

Name _____

Write the words that will make each sentence tell about the picture.

younger	fastest	smartest
livelier	most beautiful	more colorful
more upset		

---

1. The girl on the left is _____younger_____ than the girl on the right.

2. I think Mr. Martinez is the _____smartest_____ teacher in the school.

3. The baby that is crying is _____more upset_____ than the other one.

4. The painting that Joanne is holding is _____more colorful_____ than the other painting.

5. This man is the _____fastest_____ shipper at the factory.

6. Rosa is picking the _____most beautiful_____ flowers to give to her grandmother.

7. The puppy on the left is _____livelier_____ than the one on the right.

REVIEW

Read the story, and answer the questions.

The people in my family have the <u>most interesting</u> jobs. My mom is a (doctor.) She sees all kinds of patients. Some are <u>older</u> than she is. She also sees the <u>youngest</u> people in town—the babies. The people here tell us she is the <u>most trusted</u> (doctor) in town.

My dad is a famous (sculptor.) He gives art shows in our town and in the city. The shows in the city are <u>bigger</u>. My dad likes to speak with the people who come to look at his work. He is one of the <u>liveliest</u> (speakers) around. The people in our town go to his shows both here and in the city. They say my dad makes them feel famous, too, because he lives in their town.

I wonder what job I will have when I grow up. I might be a house (painter,) like my Aunt. Or, I could be a symphony (conductor,) like Grandpa. Maybe my choice will be <u>clearer</u> to me when I get to middle school!

Possible responses are shown.

1. What would be a good title for this story?

   <u>Different Kinds of Jobs</u>

2. What do the people in the town say about their doctor?

   <u>She is the most trusted doctor in town.</u>

3. What does the storyteller say about deciding what job to have?

   <u>Maybe the choice will be clearer in middle school.</u>

Now underline the words in the story that compare. Circle the words that tell what kind of job a person has.

Name _____

slowly	sugarless	farmer	impossible
editor	nonsense	painter	portable
most	cheerful		

1. The turtle moved along _____slowly_____.

2. Sheri always has a smile and a _____cheerful_____ word for everyone.

3. We watched the _____painter_____ mix the colors and get the brushes ready.

4. The _____editor_____ checked the writer's spelling.

5. I like silly cartoons, comic strips, and other _____nonsense_____.

6. My dentist says to try to eat _____sugarless_____ snacks for healthy teeth.

7. My mom says that few things are _____impossible_____ if you try your hardest.

8. We have a _____portable_____ crib for my baby sister to use when we go places.

9. That surprise party was the _____most_____ thoughtful thing anyone has ever done for me.

10. Todd's uncle is a _____farmer_____ in Texas.

Write the word that matches the definition.

| washable | rewrite | actor | thankful |
| improper | prepay | disappear | unsafe |

1. able to be washed _____washable_____

2. full of thanks _____thankful_____

3. the opposite of *appear* _____disappear_____

4. to pay before getting something _____prepay_____

5. not safe _____unsafe_____

6. not proper _____improper_____

7. to write again _____rewrite_____

8. a person who acts _____actor_____

Write the word that completes each sentence.

| deepest | sharper | more | most |

9. The river is at its _____deepest_____ just before the waterfall.

10. My blue pencil is _____sharper_____ than my yellow one.

11. This is the _____most_____ beautiful flower I have ever seen.

12. Chocolate ice cream is _____more_____ popular than strawberry.

Harcourt Brace School Publishers

Cumulative Review of Prefixes, Suffixes,
Comparatives and Superlatives, and Agents

Phonics Practice Book

Name _____

Fill in the circle next to the word that best completes each sentence. Then write the word.

1	The ___*painter*___ of this picture is my brother Frank.	○ plumber ○ painter ○ farmer
2	Mandy ___*dislikes*___ peas.	○ dislikes ○ unlike ○ likely
3	We talked to our ___*teacher*___ after class.	○ donor ○ plumber ◉ teacher
4	Marc watched a movie ___*preview*___ .	○ viewable ○ viewer ○ preview
5	Pearls are of ___*greater*___ value than pebbles.	○ greater ○ greatest ○ great
6	Our ___*nonstop*___ plane made no stops at all.	○ stoppable ○ stops ◉ nonstop
7	Do you know where the ___*coldest*___ place on Earth is?	○ cold ○ colder ◉ coldest
8	Josh puts only ___*washable*___ clothes into the washer.	○ rewash ○ wash ◉ washable
9	Amy thinks soccer is ___*more*___ fun than basketball.	○ most ○ more ○ not

Phonics Practice Book

Prefixes, Suffixes, Comparatives and Superlatives, and Word Endings Test

Read the story. Then fill in the circle next to the best answer for each question.

I love to hear Grandma retell stories she heard when she was young. Some things are impossible to believe, but they are fun to hear anyway. Grandma's stories are full of interesting people who do silly things. I don't think Grandma would really say anything untrue, but sometimes she stretches things a little bit.

Grandma is a wonderful storyteller. As she speaks, she changes her voice to sound like different people. And she comes up with the most remarkable props. She can quickly fold a piece of paper to become a ship or a hat— whatever her story needs.

Most of Grandma's stories don't seem preplanned. I think she just makes them up as she goes along. The saddest part of the day at Grandma's is when she has to discontinue the storytelling and I have to go to bed!

1 What would be a good title for this story?	○ Grandma's Special Stories ○ The Darkest Night ○ When the Writer Preplans	
2 What must be true if Grandma's stories are *not* preplanned?	○ Grandma plans them ahead of time. ◉ Grandma makes them up as she goes along. ○ She writes them down before she tells them.	
3 What is the saddest part of the day at Grandma's?	○ when she calls the children in for supper ○ when she goes to work ◉ when she discontinues the storytelling	

Prefixes, Suffixes, Comparatives and Superlatives, and Word Endings Test

Phonics Practice Book

Harcourt Brace School Publishers

Before School

Before school, Jed gets the eggs after he has fed the hens. Then he takes the eggs back to his dad.

Now it's your turn! Tell and show something you do before school.

Before school, Meg takes Rags out for as long as she can. Then Rags does not feel so sad when Meg is at school.

Directions: Help your child cut and fold the book.

Cut-Out Fold-Up Book I • Short Vowels: *a, e*

Before school, Nan lets her pet cat sit on her lap for a while. Then the cat might not feel so alone all day.

Good Morning! It's time to get up. There are things to do before school, so get out of bed right now!

Fold

Fold

Harcourt Brace School Publishers

Before school, Ben helps the others get something to eat. Then he puts the jams, cans, and bags away.

Before school, Pat helps her mother get set to go to work. Mother likes to say, "Pat, you are the best yet!"

Cut-Out Fold-Up Book I • Short Vowels: *a, e*

Directions: Help your child cut and fold the book.

Getting Rid of FOX

1

"I'm keeping away from Fox," said Hen. "He comes around my hut a lot these days. I'm a bit afraid of him."

3

"You are the BEST!" said Hen. She gave them all a hug and a kiss. What do you think Hen will do next?

8

Buzz! Down came the flying Bat! Pop! Up jumped the big Dog. Zip! Out came Duck, nipping at Fox!

9

Directions: Help your child cut and fold the book.

4

"The next time you
see Fox, ask him in,"
said Dog. "We'll help
you get rid of Fox
for good."

Dog, Duck, and
Bat came up.
"Why are you up
there, Hen?"
they asked.

Hen was sitting on
top of her hut.

2

— Fold —

— Fold —

Later, Hen said, "Come in, Fox!"
Fox licked his lips. He was thinking,
"At last, I'm in luck!"

1

5

"Help!" Fox ran
away, huffing and
puffing.
He never came
back. Bat, Dog, and
Duck got rid
of Fox for good.

7

Fold - Up Book 2

Directions: Help your child cut and fold the book.

Jean's Painting

Miss Clay said, "Go out and take a peek. Then, in painting class, you can sketch and paint what you have seen."

Fold

Harcourt Brace School Publishers

Here is Jean's painting. This time, no one asked, "What is it?" How do you think Jean feels now? Why?

8

"Wait," said Dave. "Why can't you take some real leaves? You could paste the leaves on your sheet and then—"

Directions: Help your child cut and fold the book.

Cut-Out Fold-Up Book 3 • Long Vowels: *a, e*

It was a very pretty day. Outside, the leaves on the trees were turning from green to red.

Fold

"Yes!" said Jean. "I could show a tree branch with leaves. I think I could sketch the branch, at least."

Harcourt Brace School Publishers

When they were outside, Jean wailed, "I hate painting class!"
"Why? What do you mean?" said Dave.

Fold

Jean said, "My paintings never look right. When I did one of a sheep last week, everyone said, 'What is it?'"

 298

Cut-Out Fold-Up Book 3 • Long Vowels: *a, e*

Directions: Help your child cut and fold the book.

Nine Limes

These nine green limes who loved to gloat,
Boasted every day in their home by a boat.

3

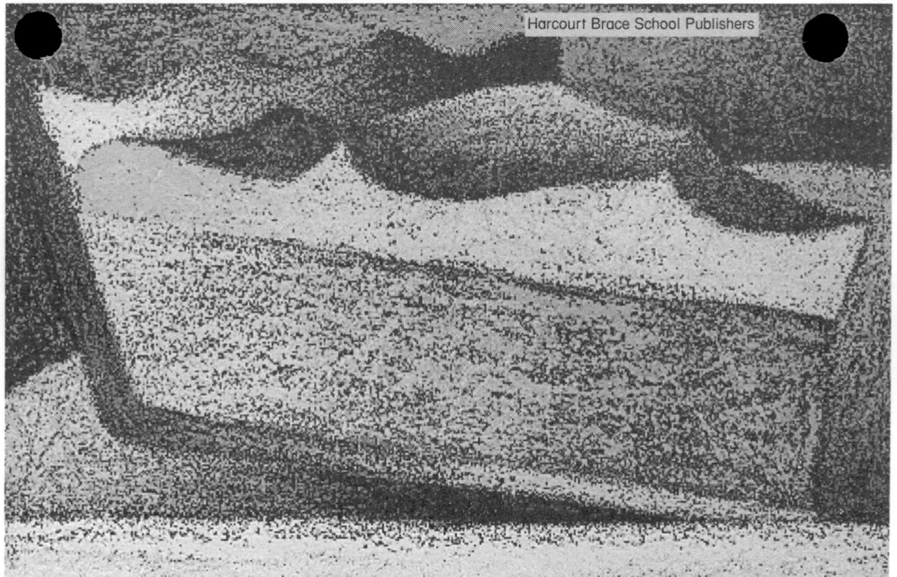

You see those nine sliced limes made a beautiful pie.
"Won't you have a slice? Come on, give it a try."

8

Harcourt Brace School Publishers

"We're nine huge limes, so full of pride.
Our rind is so beautiful, why should we hide?"

6

Directions: Help your child cut and fold the book.

4

"We're nine cute limes, watch us grow.
We're ripe and fat, don't you know?"

2

Here are nine little limes sitting in a tree,
Soaking up the sun and humming with the bees.

Fold

Fold

So those nine silly limes, they laughed all day.
Even the bugs and the birds all ran away.

5

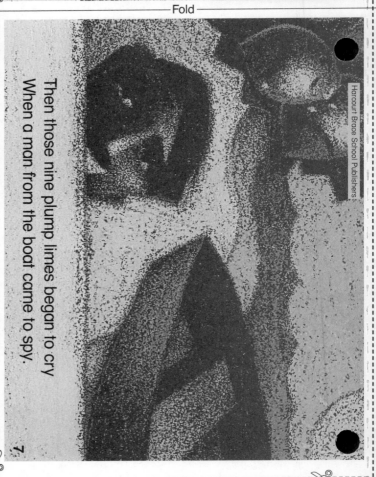

7

Then those nine plump limes began to cry
When a man from the boat came to spy.

Harcourt Brace School Publishers

Directions: Help your child cut and fold the book.

CARP

They like to slurp insects and worms from rivers. Their strong tails swish back and forth in the ferns and grass.

2

3

When the wind blows, it looks like the carp are swimming hard—just like they do in the water.

Harcourt Brace School Publishers

8

In Japan, carp are very important because they have energy and power. Some people keep carp in their gardens. The carp may be orange, white, and black.

9

Directions: Help your child cut and fold the book.
Phonics Practice Book

Cut-Out Fold-Up Book 5 • R-Controlled Vowels

301

Some carp live on fish farms and become
quite large—nearly three feet long!

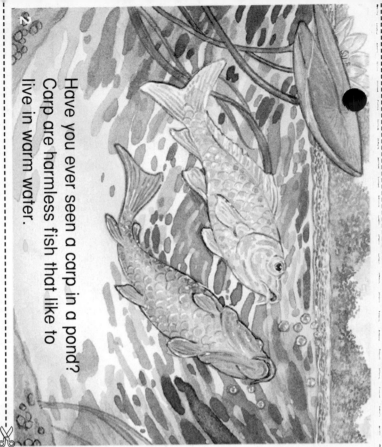

Have you ever seen a carp in a pond?
Carp are harmless fish that like to
live in warm water.

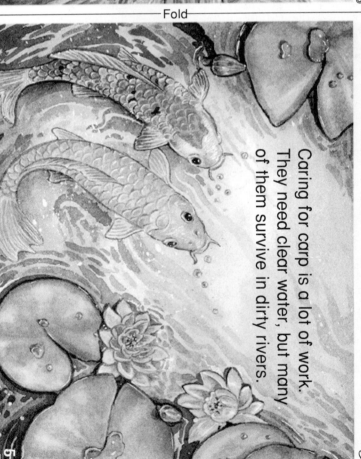

Caring for carp is a lot of work.
They need clear water, but many
of them survive in dirty rivers.

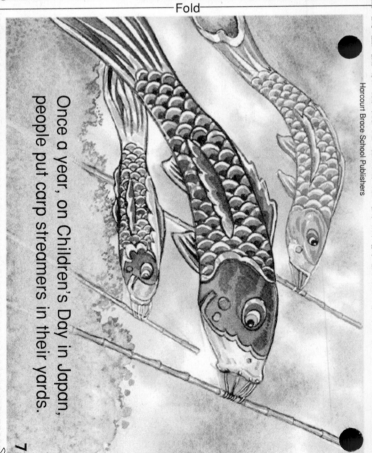

Once a year, on Children's Day in Japan,
people put carp streamers in their yards.

Harcourt Brace School Publishers

Cut-Out Fold-Up Book 5 • R-Controlled Vowels

Directions: Help your child cut and fold the book.
Phonics Practice Book

Batty Bloom's **MOOD**

Her friends' laughter didn't change her mood. "Cheer up, Bitty. Have some food," said Drew.

Draw a picture to show what you think Bitty Bloom did.

"That gives me an idea," Bitty thought. "I know what would work!"

8

6

3

"Don't be blue, Bitty," said Floyd. "Let's give Bitty our Noisy Cheer," they said.

2

Bitty Bloom was a clown with a problem. She could not stop frowning.

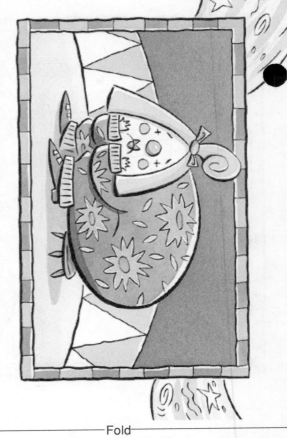

Fold

Fold

Bitty found her costume and props. "This will change my mood."

Harcourt Brace School Publishers

"Turn around! Touch the ground! Walk on your hands! Make them laugh! Make them howl! Sing with the band!"

5

7

Directions: Help your child cut and fold the book.

Cut-Out Fold-Up Book 6 • Vowel Diphthongs and Vowel Variants

Phonics Practice Book